HQ

303018127 5

D0831071

THE LIONS
South Africa 2009
HSBC

WALES
PLAY IN RED

WALES
PLAY IN RED

The Rugby Diaries of Carolyn Hitt

Gomer

Published in 2012 by
Gomer Press, Llandysul, Ceredigion, SA44 4JL

ISBN 978 1 84851 564 2

A CIP record for this title is available from the British Library

© text: Carolyn Hitt
© photographs: Huw Evans Picture Agency (unless otherwise stated)

This book is published with the financial support of the
Welsh Books Council

Printed and bound in Wales at
Gomer Press, Llandysul, Ceredigion

Contents

Page 20

Page 49

Page 57

Page 79

Page 111

Page 123

Page 166

Page 142

Acknowledgements

A massive thank you to Ceri Wyn Jones at Gomer for giving me the privilege of writing this book and steering me through the process with such expertise, enthusiasm… and patience. Thanks to Gari Lloyd and the design team for making it look so lovely and the Huw Evans Picture Agency for providing such great photographic illustration. I'm also grateful to Sioned Wyn and Riot Communications for all their help in promoting *Wales Play In Red*, and for the assistance of the Welsh Books Council.

Thank you to Simon Farrington who persuaded me to write about rugby in the first place back in 1999, and Alan Edmunds and all his *Western Mail* staff who have given my copy such a wonderful platform for so many years. I am particularly grateful to the *Western Mail*'s regular rugby correspondents Simon Thomas and Andy Howell and BBC Online's Gareth Roberts who have always been hugely helpful, from technical tips to ensuring I haven't got lost in stadiums across two hemispheres. Thanks too to Alan Evans who introduced me to writing about the Welsh club scene and gave me my first experience of match programme notes.

Thank you for the encouragement, reassurance and advice I have received from rugby journalists I greatly admire – including Rob Cole, Peter Corrigan, Peter Jackson, Gerald Davies, Alun Wyn Bevan, Brendan Gallagher, Gareth Charles, Huw Llewelyn Davies, Stephen Jones, Steve James and John Hopkins – and the support of so many legendary players and personalities who have put up with my requests for quotes and insights – including Gareth Edwards, Clive Rowlands, Max Boyce, Ray Williams, Matthew Rhys, Rhodri Morgan, Barry John, Phil Bennett, David Watkins, Scott Gibbs, Jonathan Davies, John Dawes and Cliff Morgan.

Thank you to Dennis Gethin, David Pickering, Roger Lewis, John Williams, Simon Rimmer, Gemma James and Craig Maxwell of the Welsh Rugby Union for allowing me privileged access to so many rugby people, places and stories.

Thank you to my fellow tourists who've helped me collect colour from all over the world and brought unparalleled glamour to the annual Welsh Rugby Writers Dinner. Let's hear it for The Hitt Squad (Karen Price, Jenny Johnson, Danielle Hitt, Ceri Gould, Justine Pickering, Jan Gethin, Dot Davies, Joanne Scannell, Elaine Craig, Louise Cole, Eleri Twynog Davies, Hannah Thomas, Kate Cockbain and Karen Thornton).

And finally thank you to my lovely father Bill. You may be my sternest critic but you're also the only person who has meticulously filed a cutting of every piece I've ever written. And if you hadn't done that Dad this book would never have happened.

Carolyn Hitt

I've always loved the careful and crafted consideration given to the titles of books and songs and the immediate effect they have on the reader or prospective buyer. What alchemy is at work that decides which book a reader takes from the library shelves with each one as worthy as the next? *Wales Play In Red* is a brilliantly conceived title and, like the book itself, conjures up all sorts of images and thoughts, both real and imagined, and whose secrets only the turning page can reveal.

The celebrated French poet Baudelaire wrote of an artist unknown: 'Many a gem, the poet mourns, abides forgotten in the dust, unnoticed there/Many a rose regretfully confides the secrets of its scent to empty air'. I for one am glad these vignettes will not rest unnoticed and forgotten, *Western Mail*-ed on some dark shelf, for they are little journeys, fond memories recalled and worth visiting like old friends. They deserve to be shared, for only then can their true worth be realised.

The world this book inhabits is a place where rugby football plays no mean part. That special place, with its unique camaraderie, has thrown up more than its fair share of characters and humour – captured so beautifully and accurately here. And surely it has a claim for literary permanence.

Many will recognise themselves with shame and joy in these hilarious accounts for they have walked the same path and travelled the same journey to a similar place and time, often in far and distant lands. I have had the pleasure of accompanying Carolyn on only part of the way, but it is something I will always fondly remember.

They were pilgrimages of hope and happiness, sometimes sadness and despair. But all ultimately driven by the insatiable need to see Wales play in red.

Max Boyce
October 2012

The late Mervyn Davies during his
final International match for Wales,
against France in Cardiff, 1976

(Colorsport)

Primary school eisteddfod 1976. 'Draw a picture that means Wales to you,' said our headmaster. Carol Andrew drew a daffodil. Sara Ellis drew a pit-head wheel. And me? I drew Mervyn Davies.

Rugby was always a family obsession. My older brothers would head for the Arms Park on international day and I'd ask to go with them. They used the same excuse to leave me behind each time, creating a forbidding male aura around the national stadium. 'You can't come, you'd just get peed on,' they'd say dismissively. When I finally did sit in the West Stand, I brought an umbrella, just in case.

So I stayed at home to watch the Five Nations on the television with my parents. Curtains drawn to prevent rays of winter sunshine hitting the screen, slap-up lunch of sausage, beans and chips on the coffee table and the sound of my mother shrieking 'Geddit it out! Geddit it out!' every time a ruck was formed.

But as a grown-up journalist, I never wrote about rugby until I had a phone call in 1999. 'We want you to do a column on the world cup – a woman's view,' said the *Western Mail*'s deputy editor. 'We've got Ieuan Evans, J.J. Williams, Gavin Hastings, Bill McLaren – and you.' Blimey, I thought, I'm the only one who isn't a Grogg. There was just one small snag. It was too late to get a press pass. I mentioned my ticket dilemma in the first column. By lunchtime, I'd been offered five. And so the adventure began.

I enjoyed the column so much I never stopped, climbing aboard Welsh rugby's rollercoaster and hanging on for dear life through giddy heights, swooping lows and the thrilling ride towards Wales's first Grand Slam in 27 years with one more thrown in for good measure three years later and yet another in 2012. Not to mention the world cup that made the world want to be Welsh.

I've witnessed a generation of players say hello and goodbye, smiling at the first appearance of a cherubic Shane Williams in his Welsh trial match, weeping at his final fling 11 years later. I've chronicled the game outside the game, the politics, the celebrity, the inexorable rise of fake tan.

And I've written reams on the ordinary lovers of the game too – although what goes on tour doesn't necessarily stay on tour when I've been following the adventures of fans across the world, I have forged a bond of trust with the Welsh supporter. So when a bunch of middle-aged men from Gilfach Goch say 'Please don't mention the stopover in Bangkok cos the wives don't know, see love', I'm happy to oblige.

Along the way, I've never been stuck for intriguing subject matter. From Henry's Heroes to Ruddock's Dragons to Gareth Jenkins's Welsh Way to Gatland's Young Guns,

Spot the one who isn't a Grogg? *(Carolyn Hitt)*

it's been a period that has seen seismic change on and off the pitch. I hope I've reflected the excitement of that journey in this anthology – which draws on my experiences of three world cups, two Lions Tours, 12 Six Nations campaigns across Europe and quite a few damp Friday nights at Stradey, Sardis Road and Cardiff Arms Park.

So I'd like to think in oval ball terms, I've made a few small steps for a Welsh woman, but the odd giant leap for Welsh womankind. I'm the first female on the committee of the Welsh Rugby Writers Association. They even gave me a tie. But perhaps most importantly, I've made lasting friendships from Murrayfield to Melbourne and been privileged to say I Was There for some truly thrilling moments in the recent history of Welsh rugby.

Being often the only woman in the press box has had its moments. On being introduced to a former senior WRU blazer as 'one of the few female rugby writers' his retort was: 'Yes, but can she read a map?' Yet the welcome has always been warm from my male colleagues, particularly in the early days when they showed commendable patience in dealing with my constant refrain of 'wassat for?' each time the ref's whistle blew. The banter has produced the title of this book. Rob Cole, director of Westgate Sports Agency, makes the same quip every time I leave the Press Room of the Millennium Stadium to take my seat in the stand: 'Just remember – Wales play in red.'

But gender plays no part in the one thing that unites the fan and the journalist – the love of the game. For me, there's an added passion. Writing about rugby is writing about

Wales itself. Its red thread is woven into the fabric of our identity. I couldn't separate rugby from my sense of Welshness in the school eisteddfod of 1976 and I can't divide them now. That's why I love writing about this game.

My mother, June, loved it too. When we watched games together, she provided more commentary than Jonathan Davies. The week Wales began their 2011 world cup campaign she was diagnosed with cancer. She saw the feelgood factor of Wales's journey through the tournament as a welcome distraction from her tests and treatment. Likewise the Grand Slam, which she managed to enjoy despite her increasingly fragile health.

She died on March 31, 2012. She was a passionate supporter of Welsh rugby, my biggest fan and the best Mam I could have wished for. *Wales Play In Red* is dedicated to her memory.

On tour with Mam and Dad   *(Carolyn Hitt)*

Chapter 1

Grand Slam Diaries 2005

*I encourage them to enjoy the game
and play rugby with a smile.*
Mike Ruddock

. . . .

Everyone had a Prayer in Six Nations Broad Church

*F*or the press pack, the Six Nations countdown begins in earnest each year at the official launch in January. In 2005 there was none of the usual nonsense predicting a two-horse race between England and France. Everyone sensed this could be the most open contest in the history of the tournament. And Wales had already impressed the previous autumn, losing to New Zealand by a single point. Could this be the end of a 27-year wait for glory?

RUGBY has always been a religion in Wales but the launch of the RBS 2005 Six Nations was more C of E than chapel. Indeed, it was pretty high church, staged in an ecclesiastical conference centre in the shadows of Westminster Abbey. In the narrow streets surrounding Church House, women priests shopped for new robes in J Wippell, outfitters to the clergy. Inside, the sweat-resistant Lycra vestments were less Vicar of Dibley. As cherubic choristers played football in the Dean's Yard, the six captains assembled for a photo. Gareth Thomas's broad grin and stitched eyebrow ensured he looked the naughtiest altar boy.

The coaches sang hymns of praise to the opposition. Saint Jonny was brought out first for media adoration. Before the softly-spoken talisman could hand down his thoughts on Wales v England, however, we had to talk about The Injury. Wilkinson looked as fed up of discussing his knees as anyone outside the English press was, but fielded questions with his usual earnest patience and articulacy. At the mention of the threat posed by Wales, he perked up, sounding genuinely impressed by their pace and skill.

Reigning Grand Slam champions France were next. Bernard Laporte and the brooding presence of Fabien Pelous, a Gallic doppelganger for Desperate Dan. Laporte delivered his verdict in Frenglish. 'We can't discount any team,' he shrugged, 'Welsh is coming up, Ireland played well but we try to conserve the trophy.' Like injury-ravaged England, Les Blues squad resembled an episode of *Holby City*, but when asked if he still had the players to win a third Grand Slam, Laporte was adamant: 'Sure!' he declared.

Italy coach John Kirwan's sights were set a little lower but the man who mixed Kiwi grit with the Latin charm of his adopted country was seeking help from an expert at delivering the goods. He advised his players to think of themselves as children again, and await the gifts that Santa Claus can provide. 'I have told them to believe in him and to go to bed early on the eve of a match and not do anything bad, and they can awake at the end of the tournament and hopefully he has delivered one or two presents... in our parlance: victories.' Kirwan's paternal theme continued as he described how he explains the concept of the necessary pain that comes before success to his players. 'I smacked my son on the arm the other day.

He said "Ow, what did you do that for?" but he hadn't seen the mosquito.' There were no metaphorical flourishes when Kirwan was asked about the opposition: 'Wales are the most improved team.'

Ireland's Eddie O'Sullivan also had his eye on the Cymric dark horse: 'Wales have really ruffled a few feathers. If they continue in that vein they are suddenly pushing.'

Scotland coach Matt Williams made no mention of Wales's prospects, but that season he had enough to worry about. Gareth Thomas and Mike Ruddock had plenty to say. Alfie was in slick media-speak mode until he brought the house down with a verbal slip. 'Team spirit is fantastic. The players all get off with each other', he said. 'I mean *on*, I mean *on*!' he laughed, as the room erupted.

The message taken home from Church House was England, France, Ireland and Wales all had a prayer that year. Just don't forget God is Welsh…

January 29, 2005

The Day Elvis was Alive and Kicking

Nursing a monumental hangover from celebrating Wales's victory over England, I sat in front of the computer on the Sunday morning still grinning but wondering where on earth to start. The phone rang. It was the Western Mail *news editor. 'Just write about Henson,' she said. 'As much as you like.' So I did.*

February 5, 2005 **Wales 11 England 9**

On February 5, 2005, the boy who looks like Elvis shook, rattled and rolled over England and sent them packing back to their Heartbreak Hotel. For blue suede shoes, read silver leather. For Brylcreemed quiffs, read gelled spikes. And the King probably never shaved his legs. But with a kick that would clinch victory for Wales a few metres in from the right touchline and 44 metres out, Gavin Henson was about to enter rock god territory.

As soon as the penalty was given, the chant spread through the crowd: 'Henson! Henson! Henson!' Stephen Jones had first refusal but told captain Gareth Thomas it was not within his range. 'I looked at Gav and he gave me a reassuring nod,' Alfie revealed later. We'd waited 12 years for that silver-booted kick to end the Old Enemy's dominance in Cardiff. Five minutes to go and a last chance of glory. Yet how many times had we been in this position before only for Lady Luck to give the Harvey Smith salute?

But among the 74,197 knotted stomachs, bitten nails and eyes peeping through fingers, one 23-year-old felt no pressure. His pre-kick ritual was simple. No elaborate hand clasping,

15

'I knew I was going to get it…'
Gavin Henson kicks Wales to victory

or muttered prayers. Its only quirk was the usual flick of the foot before toe made contact with ball. Time seemed to stretch as the ball arced towards the post. The roar began before it dropped sweetly over the crossbar. It was never in doubt. 'I knew I was going to get it before I even took the kick,' Henson said, almost indignant that anyone should think otherwise. 'I have been getting them from that distance all year so it wasn't a problem. I had to deliver and I think I did.'

An intense midfield battle had been predicted. England had built up their own centre of attention, teenage debutant Matthew Tait. Endorsed by the absent talisman Jonny Wilkinson – 'I never knew what the phrase "someone really special" meant until I saw him in action' – great things were expected of the Newcastle youngster. But Henson had arranged a one-man welcoming-committee to the brutal world of international rugby, spectacularly upending him twice. The second time, he cradled Tait in his arms for a moment as if to underline he was the infant on the pitch. Unfortunately for Tait, in this instance King Herod was babysitting.

In a game devoid of beauty, Henson brought elegance in attack and grit in defence. He seemed to create a bubble of space and time around him, stealing extra seconds for a whopping kick to touch or a deft show and go. His facial expressions ranged from nonchalant to impassive – he'd only allow himself a smile if he did something really special. While the rest of the team were pictured in training, grinning and cracking jokes, Henson publicity shots resembled the portfolio of an Armani model.

Which brought us to the image. The way he looked drew the eye almost as much as the way he played. Fortunately, one did not detract from the other. As Jeremy Guscott pointed out, 'For a pretty boy he certainly puts in the tackles'. The grooming of Welsh rugby players had improved greatly since Bob Norster was the first forward to bring hair gel into the dressing room, but Henson had taken it to a whole new level. He was an unashamed metrosexual, maintaining a burnished glow in the depths of a Neath winter and skewering his locks into ever more complex spike formations. Retail therapy loomed large in his extra-curricular life.

'I do like my shopping, mind; I like to look smart,' he once admitted, before revealing trips to the Body Shop for facial products and detailing his latest purchase, 'a Dolce & Gabbana jumper, £150, black with a bit of red, it's quite nice.'

The fashion sense extended to the pitch. Like the trendy sixth former who customises his school uniform, Henson accessorised his Welsh kit with his trademark precious metal footwear. As for the hair removal that made the headlines, yes, shaving your legs does make you more slippery in the tackle, but it also emphasises the tan and muscle definition.

But the great irony of Henson's attention-grabbing appearance was he was actually quite shy. He possessed a confidence in his ability that bordered on arrogance – which is no bad thing – yet away from the game he had to work on his social skills. Former Swansea coach John Connolly came up with a way for Henson to conquer his timidity. Each morning as he

• •

arrived at the club, Connolly made him go into the office to talk to people and bring him out of himself.

Family remained 23-year-old Henson's touchstone. 'They're the only people I can really talk to. They've always believed in me. When I had poor school reports they wouldn't mind, they saw my caps as GCSEs or A-levels – they always believed I was going to make it in rugby because that's all I've ever wanted to do.' When I interviewed Henson about his ambitions as a nineteen-year-old, he saw rugby as a way of helping his parents enjoy an easier life. His mother, Audrey, helped his father, Alan, run a felt-roofing business. 'My father is working too hard, he needs to stop, I need to make some money to make him retire. I've worked for him for a year during my GCSE year and it was harder than anything I've ever done before. He's doing that every day. It would be nice to sort him out so he wouldn't have to do that for much longer.'

The Henson family were steeped in rugby – both his father and grandfather played for Maesteg and the five-year-old Henson played for Pencoed Under-Eights, staying with the club until he was 16. After his first Six Nations match, the nation now shared the pride they felt in him. Of course, the Welsh victory was a massive team effort. As Gareth Thomas pointed out: 'Gavin was superb but I hope the emphasis in the press will be that the whole team should take the credit, and I'm sure Gav would be the first person to agree with me on that. It's crucial we stick together.'

Yet sport occasionally throws up a figure whose combination of talent and image ensure his appeal transcends the field of play. It's common in football, rarer in rugby. Henson represented that sort of alchemy. However unfair it may be in the realms of team sport, the media thrives on individual icons. At the post-match press conference various players were made available for interview. As it became apparent that Henson wasn't on the list, the Wales team press officer found himself under siege from protesting hacks. 'He's only doing *GQ* magazine,' quipped one.

But would Henson-mania taint the object of our affection? Adulation sometimes brings an unwelcome friend in rugby. Soccer accommodates its Prada-clad pin-ups with ease, but the oval ball game was still wary of those it considers to be a bit of a poseur. Brian O'Driscoll, the most sublime gift to Irish rugby, had copped an unbelievable amount of flak in his homeland for his supposed celebrity lifestyle and flowing highlighted locks.

But we let Henson enjoy his moment in the sun. We certainly did. That Monday morning in Wales hadn't felt so good for a long time. The band was fantastic but the spotlight belonged to the lead singer. And after the kick that put the boot in England's 12-year unbeaten run in Cardiff, setting us off on what would prove to be a very exciting journey, we couldn't help falling in love with the boy who looked like Elvis.

February 7, 2005

18

● ●

A Taste of La Dolce Vita for the Red Army

February 12, 2005 **Italy 8 Wales 38**

La Vita was tasting pretty dolce on the streets of the Italian capital. The Red Army celebrated two on the trot for Wales with their usual brio. When in Rome, act as Welsh as possible is still the attitude of the travelling fans. The locals, who glide from pavement cafe to pizzeria in their stylish Euro uniform of tweed, leather and designer shades must think everyone in Wales is surgically attached to an inflatable daffodil. Apart from Our Gavin, of course, who would look perfectly at home nipping down Via Cavour on the back of a Vespa, gelled spikes immobile in the wind.

Even before the six-try rout at Stadio Flaminio, those on tour arrived in celebratory mood. The sparkle of the previous weekend's victory had not dimmed. Six-year-old supporter Will Haynes was literally jumping for joy as he clutched his little backpack at Cardiff Airport in the early hours of Friday morning. 'He's watched Wales before but this is his first away trip,' explained his grandmother Margaret Williams, as the beaming youngster bounced towards the check-in.

On the plane, fiftysomething couple Tessa and Paul Price were enjoying a rare break from running their dairy farm in Gelligaer. Toasting their first rugby trip to Rome with a 7am Bacardi and Coke, Paul described how he had to give his Wales v England tickets away after falling ill. 'I gave them to a mate. I owed him a favour as he'd given me a nice bull. He brought an English friend with him, which made him enjoy the match even more,' said Paul, who along with their rest of his gang from Penallta RFC, was planning to wear a red toga to the game.

The Friday morning Italian news bulletins showed John Paul II arriving home from hospital in his Pobe Mobile in a haze of paparazzi flash bulbs. The Holy Father had a Welsh welcoming committee in St Peter's Square, as arriving fans made a sightseeing beeline for the Vatican. Deciding not to endure the mammoth queue for the Sistine Chapel, I explored the Vatican's large souvenir emporium. It turned out to be the T K Maxx of Catholicism, with all manner of religious knick knacks for sale, from Virgin Marys in assorted sizes to personalised Papal Blessings, yours for a snip at just 35 euros. Quite what the spiritual value of the three pack of Vatican Golf Balls was, however, remained to be seen.

I bumped into Max Boyce and his wife Jean at the Metro station. As far as the Rome trip was concerned, Max was a vestal virgin. Remarkably for someone who has helped create the culture of going on tour, it was the first time the world's most famous Welsh rugby fan could say 'I Was There'. And he was loving every minute of it.

Welsh supporters enjoying an eve of game pasta supper were also treated to Clive Rowlands's rendition of '*O Sole Mio*', although his lyrics owed more to Wall's Ice Cream than

· ·

Shane Williams leaves
the Azzurri defence
grasping thin air

Di Capua. On the next table a group from Mountain Ash were discussing the effect Gavin Henson was having on their teenage daughters. Deb Polkinghorne produced a still from her digital camera of her 14-year-old daughter Jessica embracing a poster of Henson with the doe-eyed reverence her mother's generation reserved for David Cassidy. 'All of a sudden Jessica and her friends are taking a big interest in rugby,' said Deb.

On match day, the open-air bars surrounding Stadio Flaminio began to buzz two hours before kick-off. While the Welsh fans provided the usual mix of boozing, bonhomie and comedy costumes, there was also a sense that Italy was starting to embrace the Six Nations experience. Mini rugby players paraded through the crowds with Italian tricolours painted on their cheeks; banners bearing slogans from Italian rugby clubs were unfurled and every single Azzurri fan was given a blue flag to wave.

The best pre-match entertainment was provided by a trio of fortysomething ladies from Burry Port in voluminous dragon dresses. As three nubile models in miniskirts gyrated on stage to promote a new brand of Murphy's bitter, the Llanelli ladies muscled in on the performance, in the manner of the Pontypool Front Row dispatching a bunch of Nancy Boy backs. The models admitted defeat as caterer Tina Roberts, shop assistant Linda Hughes and carer Christine Evans boogied for Wales. They were joined for their finale by a stag party of Roman gladiators from Port Talbot. The groom-to-be, 35-year-old landscape gardener Simon Morgan looked a little more embarrassed in his white dress and blonde wig. 'He's Helen of Troy – the face that sank a thousand ships,' explained his friends, obviously not afraid to mix their classical references.

But, of course, the best dancing of the day came from the fleet feet of Shane Williams, whether the wondrous wing was creating or scoring tries. Brent Cockbain's debut score was a poignant delight as his teammates rushed to embrace him. Another Welsh performance to catch the breath. Yet should the nation contain its excitement, Mike Ruddock was asked afterwards. 'I said from day one I wanted this team to be exciting to coach, exciting to play in and exciting to watch,' he replied. 'If people are getting excited then it's going to plan.'

Waiting for the plane home, little Will Haynes was still bouncing with the thrill of his Roman holiday. 'He's been like that all weekend,' said his grandmother, 'especially when Shane scored.' But as Wales's Six Nations journey continued on an upward path you didn't have to be six years old to be excited.

February 14, 2005

And the Oscar goes to...

This was the match that proved Wales really were something special. They had steel as well as silken skills. It has to rank as one of the most enthralling games ever played. I was literally trembling in the last few minutes as the men in red refused to surrender. As the match coincided with the Academy Awards weekend, there was just one extended metaphor for the match report. And I'm particularly proud to have filed this one – I had to stop seven times while writing it on the Eurostar home to regurgitate the dodgy Parisien mussels I'd eaten in celebration the night before...

February 26, 2005 **France 18 Wales 24**

And the Oscar for Best Drama goes to... Wales. The screenplay bore all the hallmarks of the finest thrillers. Not one member of the 80,000-strong audience could have predicted the denouement on the evidence of the opening scenes. Narrative twists are one thing. This plot had corkscrew turns, whirling us from tragedy to triumph in the space of 80 frenzied minutes.

Yet the supporting cast of Welsh supporters were expecting nothing less than *Enter The Dragon* as they filed into Stade de France. Jauntily bouncing their inflatable daffodils to the beat of '*La Marseillaise*', and fuelled by a day's familiarity with Parisian hostelries, their expectations were higher than the Eiffel Tower.

The French crowd displayed their usual talent for mischief, casting coach Bernard Laporte as the villain with a chorus of boos and reserving the biggest cheer for Frederic Michalak, on the bench but hoping for a cameo role.

They were to witness a performance that borrowed from all the cinematic genres: romance, war movies, even a moment of Looney Tunes cartoon slapstick as strapping French wing Aurelien Rougerie pushed over Shane Williams with worrying ease. The first half made disturbing viewing. For 40 minutes France were arthouse, Wales were a video nasty.

Gallic starlet Julien Laharrague was determined to hog the spotlight in his debut role. Combining with Rougerie on mazy runs through the Welsh defence, he restored the glamour that had been missing from Les Blues' Six Nations. Their respective black and blond locks flew aerodynamically in the wind, as if to underline that French pretty boy rugby was back.

Welsh fans looked to their own stellar backline for inspiration. But at this point they seemed as static as Gavin Henson's gel-sculpted hairline. As Rougerie followed a searing path to the try line, a wrongfooted Henson was left in midfield. His silver boot slid off. It appeared the Grand Slam dream was skidding to a halt with that shiny symbol of a Welsh revival.

A close-up of Ryan Jones shaking his head in frustration filled the big screen. Central character Gareth Thomas was about to disappear from the story. Welsh supporters felt a creeping sense of déjà vu. Were we about to unravel in that all too familiar fashion? Only Stephen Jones's pair of penalties and the fact that an outrageous abundance of French territory and possession had produced a meagre 15 points offered a lifeline.

Could Wales rewrite the script?

Oh yes. It was Martyn Williams's turn to call the shots. So often the best supporting actor, providing the subtle yet vital touches that allow others to shine, he now had the spotlight to himself. And he didn't hang around. By the time I had returned to my seat for the second half, arranged my cheese baguette, notebook, pen and spare pen, Martyn was curving round behind the posts. I was still writing up Shane Williams's shimmying offload to him when he scored again. Wales were ahead, the plot took an about turn and the Stade de France soundtrack changed from Breton oompah-pah bands to a delirious rendition of 'Hymns and Arias'.

What on earth had the director said to his cast at half-time? In the realms of inspirational oratory it must have been rugby's answer to Martin Luther King's I Have A Dream speech,

Two tries from Martyn Williams turned the game for Wales in Paris

••

Henry V's pre-Agincourt rallying cry and a vintage Clive Rowlands rant rolled into one. But as Mike Ruddock later revealed with his usual unassuming charm, it was a little more prosaic than that. 'We talked about the Three Ts,' he explained, 'turnovers, tackles and missing touch.'

And crucially there was belief, embodied by the reassuring bulk and cool head of stand-in captain, Michael Owen, leading from the front and cannily opting for the quick-tap penalty that eventually led to Wales's second try. On the soil of his adopted country, Stephen Jones set the second half alight with the fire in his belly. When he chipped the deftest of drop goals to extend the Welsh lead, Jonathan Davies punched the commentary box air with joy.

'That drop goal was just sublime,' purred Mike Ruddock, 'it oozed class.' But France were still threatening to change the climax of the storyline. Michalak was given his cameo role, weaving his slightly wayward brand of magic and firing his backline. And then came the final battle. The Welsh scrum had endured a torrid time throughout but in the defining conflict they withstood the onslaught, even if they came heart-stoppingly close to conceding a penalty try in the process. After all the pre-match hype about the formidable French pack, it was a delicious paradox that Welsh forward power safeguarded victory.

Yet just when your pulse is beginning to slow with relief, no thriller is complete without one last frightener. Like a bloodied Glenn Close leaping out of the bath in the closing moments of *Fatal Attraction*, France launched themselves at the Welsh defence once more. Rougerie's hurtling run towards the try line ended in a smothering mass of red jerseys. The clock was frozen on 80 minutes but the ball was still in play until Stephen Jones spun round and hoofed it right into the heart of the Welsh supporters. It was the referee's turn to create a subplot. Giving 'dramatic pause' a whole new meaning, he waited a few more agonising seconds before blowing the whistle.

Ryan Jones ran to the embrace of his family in the crowd. Battle-scarred Kevin Morgan, sporting egg-like bumps to his face, jumped for joy, cycling his legs in the air. And after the lap of honour, man of the match Stephen Jones took the microphone and spoke in a voice filled with emotion. 'Two years ago we lost every match in the Six Nations... I'm a very proud Welshman tonight.' He wasn't the only one.

In one of the most compelling blockbusters this tournament has ever witnessed, France were content to show flashes of movie-star magic. But it is the strength of the characterisation that defines the truly great dramas. The Welsh cast contained 15 outstanding characters. As the credits rolled, every single one of them deserved star billing. And the nation just couldn't wait for the sequel.

February 28, 2005

. . . .

No Banana Skin but Plenty of Passion Fruit

*W*ales turned on the style in what was almost an exhibition match. Off the pitch, Welsh fans were also making an exhibition of themselves... particularly the girls

March 13, 2005   **Scotland 22 Wales 46**

It was billed as the potential banana skin match but Wales were the passion fruit of the Six Nations – even if they allowed Scotland to squeeze out some of their juice in the second half. For the alleged 40,000 fans who travelled north, the juice of the barley fuelled up to three days of pre-match adventures.

In the 1970s when record crowds swelled Murrayfield, supporting was still a testosterone-filled affair. This weekend showed Welsh rugby is more in touch with its feminine side than Lily Savage.

The Scottish Trip was now the ultimate Girls Night Out. Forget the usual odyssey of the boys on the bus, a coach arrived from Aberystwyth bearing 40 women and it wasn't the only one. Rose Street thronged with female chests displaying slogans that ranged from 'Ruddock's Dragons' to 'Scrum And Get It'.

Tony Lucas was hoping to exploit the female factor with a touch of entrepreneurial flair. The retired captain of the Fishguard-Rosslare ferry spent the eve of the match hawking T-shirts round the Grassmarket pubs.

'I'm doing a little market research before the Grand Slam weekend,' he explained, unveiling the design which featured a moody pic of Gavin Henson with 'Return of the Dragon' in elaborate script beneath his chin. 'My son Owen designed them. I think they'll sell like hot cakes.'

Gavin's girl, meanwhile, was making her own fashion statement. Charlotte Church, in town with mum Maria, was spotted in a cut-off Welsh rugby shirt, customised to reveal a glimpse of taut midriff. She also graced the front page of the Scottish *Sunday Times*. Her London paparazzi stalkers were led a Highland jig by Welsh snappers. Unaccustomed to the dynamics of a rugby weekend, they believed the mischievous misinformation.

'Turn up at such-a-such a field at 3pm – Charl will be there to watch Gav's kicking practice.' Yeah, right.

Not to be outdone by his other half on the grooming front, Gavin turned up for his real pre-match kicking practice sporting a new barnet. Judging by the strange feathery salt and pepper highlights sprouting from the back of his head, it would seem being an Osprey had gone quite literally to his head.

Scotland took the field accompanied by a Diddymen team of 22 mini-mascots. The roar that greeted Wales matched the volume of the home fans. The crowd of 63,431 glowed a whopping 60% red.

When the occupants of the East Stand were ordered to lift the cards beneath their seats to form a giant Scottish flag, thousands of scarlet arms stretched skywards.

'Flower of Scotland' worked its usual emotional magic. The granite features of lock Scott Murray crumpled with its final gloomy cadence. If he knew what was coming for the next 40 minutes, his tears would have filled the Firth of Forth.

For the natives, the first half was enough to make those vertigo-defying pipers throw themselves off the roof. Wales seemed to be playing an exhibition match rather than a crucial Six Nations encounter. From the moment rampaging rookie Ryan Jones started and finished the move that produced the first try, there was the sense that Ruddock's men would score every time they touched the ball.

It was intoxicating.

Forwards with softer hands than any Fairy Liquid ad could boast passed with an almost nonchalant panache while backs danced and reeled through dark blue defences. Dwayne Peel

Dwayne Peel helping Wales clock up a record score at Murrayfield

· ·

jigged around the entire Scottish pack to send Kevin Morgan on a soaring angle to the line for his second try.

Morgan left Murrayfield on a stretcher two years previously. This time he was inflicting major injuries on Scottish pride. Five tries up and birthday boy Ryan Jones – 24 the day before – was celebrating in style, Tom Shanklin was having the game of his life and Martyn Williams was once more confirming his status as the forward of the tournament.

It was almost embarrassing in a strange way. Joy for Wales was tempered by discomfort for a Celtic cousin in distress even if, curiously, many Scottish fans had admitted before the game that they wouldn't mind us winning because 'it means so much to you'. A hoarse Edinburgh accent cut through the chorus of 'Hymns and Arias', 'Come on Scotland – wake up!' But as the Welsh lead stretched to 38–3 there seemed more chance of Rip Van Winkle turning up at an all-night rave.

Yet where would this Six Nations be without the cliché of the game of two halves? Scotland woke up, smelt the coffee and drank enough of it to give Wales a decent game. There were those who left Murrayfield disappointed that Wales had not turned on their exhilarating style for 80 minutes.

But Clive Rowlands gave a sage smile and said perhaps it was the best possible psychological preparation for the Irish game. He reckoned Wales's 'poor second-half performance' was a vital 'wake-up call' that would guard against any complacency.

'I've seen them win three away games – Argentina, France and now Scotland – where they've played brilliantly for one half. Winning away makes them a very special team. Some day they'll play brilliantly in two halves. Let's hope it's next Saturday against Ireland.'

March 14, 2005

Preparing for Tomorrow's Nostalgia

The day had arrived. Wales were on the brink of Grand Slam glory. And I was feeling rather emotional…

TWENTY-SEVEN years ago my siblings tacked their *Western Mail* Souvenir Grand Slam Poster on to their bedroom wall. All those red jerseys clashed with the purple 1970s paintwork but it took pride of place alongside my 14-year-old brother's Liverpool FC pin-ups and my 16-year-old brother's signed picture of Sassafras.

Across the landing, I was growing out of Holly Hobby dolls and into John Travolta. If I'd known the Golden Era was about to expire, I'd have demanded a *Western Mail* Souvenir

26

• •

Grand Slam Poster too – we'd got it free anyway as my cousin was the printer. My brothers didn't realise then how lucky they were. Their Clearasil years were an oasis of rugby triumphs, mine were a desert of defeats.

The poster was taken down and put in the attic with the shoebox of match programmes. Occasionally, it was rediscovered and unrolled reverently like the Dead Sea Scrolls. Homage was paid to gods with moustaches and sideburns. Names were incanted – Gareth, Gerald, Benny, JPR – before the poster was rolled up once more and returned to its resting place under the eaves between the old vinyl suitcases and wooden Lego box.

Sporadically, new heroes gave us glimpses of what it must have been like for the fans a decade older than ourselves. Three years of Taffy-bashing at university by rah-rah English rugby boys was suspended for a term in 1988 when we won the Triple Crown. We clung to this achievement like Kate Winslet to a shard of Titanic flotsam until the next lifeline came along – Ieuan skinning Rory to secure that 10–9 victory over England in 1993. A championship win the following year, then the heady days of Henry's Heroes before the century turned and Wales's learning curve became a circle.

Sure we had Wembley to sustain us and we let it – to an almost embarrassing degree. In 1978 only a Grand Slam would merit a souvenir poster. In 1999 a single victory over the Old Enemy could spawn an entire nostalgia industry. I've got the video, t-shirt and jink-by-jink set of photographs recording Gibbsy's dance to the line. A generation with more 'I Was There (But I Wish I Hadn't Been)' moments than Max Boyce ever entertained in his darkest nightmare held on to Wembley as if it was a crucifix in Transylvania.

But it was difficult to keep the faith. I thought I'd reached my lowest ebb as a fan with the defeat in Dublin that saw the Great Redeemer make a sharp exit. That was until we lost against Italy and went on to endure a Six Nations whitewash the following year. All this against a backdrop of political wrangling that would make the Court of the Borgias seem a warm and relaxing place.

Yet through all this bleakness, the spark that is quintessentially *Welsh* rugby was never truly extinguished. It could be seen in the maverick moves of Mark Ring; the anthem tears of Paul Thorburn before he hoofed a record-breaking penalty; the sheer audacity of a sneaked Jonathan Davies try; the valley commando grit of Neil Jenkins; the intensity of Rob Howley; the passion of Scott Quinnell… and the shimmying of Little Shane.

On a sultry night in Sydney, Shane helped re-ignite that spark as Hansen's supposed second string tied New Zealand in world cup knots. The excitement we feel about this team today can be traced back to that match. That was the night we remembered we were Welsh. Not that anyone in the Telstra Stadium saw it coming. When the All Blacks scored within two minutes of kick off, I trudged off to fetch the chips and beers to avoid the pain. Cheer after cheer floated down to the bar. It was only when I returned to my seat 20 minutes later to see

· ·

Max Boyce practically cart-wheeling through the stand that I realised the hysteria was for Wales.

A week later in Brisbane, I had tears in my eyes watching Colin Charvis gather his men into a huddle at the final whistle, telling them how close they had come. England staggered into the semi-finals after a heroic challenge from Wales.

More glorious defeats followed but with Ruddock at the helm, belief, momentum and the Welsh way of play grew. It was only a matter of time before we put the silver boot in and brought ourselves to the brink of something golden. This team has given us so much over the past seven weeks. A victory against the world champions sealed with a nerveless kick from rugby's newest icon. A six-try rout in Rome that included the poignant sight of Brent Cockbain being embraced by the entire team and his later admission that he hoped Toby, the baby son he lost to cancer, watched him score his first try for Wales. The epic fight back in France that proved the side has steel as well as silken skills. The exquisite choreography of Murrayfield – rugby, the new ballet. And while the nation has gone into Grand Slam overdrive, the only swelling of the players' heads occurred when Kevin Morgan copped a nasty bump in Paris. Confident yes, arrogant no.

Whatever happens today, it's been a joy to be Welsh in recent weeks and the joy of Welshness has returned to the national game. Thanks to Ruddock's Dragons, the misty-eyed focus on the past is switching to the future. We no longer have to gaze wistfully at ancient Groggs or stick *The Crowning Years* in the video. A whole new generation is stacking up the rugby memories that will become tomorrow's nostalgia. I just hope there'll be a new poster on my brothers' sons' bedroom walls next week.

March 19, 2005

And the End was Just the Beginning

March 19, 2005 **Wales 32 Ireland 20**

It was never in doubt. Seven weeks previously, on the day Wales began their Six Nations campaign against England, I drove down Westgate Street at 7.15am en route to Radio Wales's Morning of the Match show at the Angel Hotel. The streets that would be thronged with red-jerseyed revellers a few hours hence, were bare. Dawn was breaking. The Millennium Stadium's corner spires were silhouetted against a morning sky streaked with gold.

It was such a beautiful spectacle. That well-worn image that had been applied so many times in desperate hope over the past 27 years – a New Dawn for Welsh rugby – was there, rising quite literally over the home of the national game. Surely it was an omen I told my friends, who laughed at the wonderful corniness of it all. Only Welsh fans could wrap their

• •

hopes up in such sentiment. But at that moment on Westgate Street I knew this new dawn would not be false. It was destiny. Wales would win the Grand Slam.

The day Wales ended their Six Nations campaign, however, began not with a wistful appreciation of first light but an early wake-up call.

'Is it sunny in Cardiff? It's glorious in Glynneath.'

It was the voice of Boyce. Favourable weather conditions in the capital were crucial to Max's revised 'Hymns and Arias' lyrics.

'Dunno, haven't looked yet.'

'You're not still in bed are you? Get up, it's match day!'

It was glorious in Cardiff too. Perfect spring sunshine for the ticketless thousands who queued on pub pavements or gathered at Henson's Hill for the big screen. The city centre was a combination of carnival, Bacchanalian feast and eisteddfod. Welsh rugby's renaissance was definitely having a positive choral impact. All three verses of '*I Bob Un Sydd Fyddlon*' haven't been heard in the Queen's Vaults for a generation.

The T-shirt slogans were ever more imaginative – we've come a long way from Valley Girl. The Brains logo had been replaced by the word 'Dreams' (can come true) on some, while other chests saucily proclaimed they had Baps of Heaven. Not that this most female of Six Nations was just about the Scrum-and-Get-It babes. Grandmothers, little girls, middle-aged women and young mums pushing face-painted toddlers in their strollers joined the party.

Irish fans were not outdone in the rugby fancy-dress stakes. There were enough leprechauns in town to fill a sequel to *Finian's Rainbow*. As the team buses ploughed their way through the masses, Irish coach Eddie O'Sullivan was struck by the wonder that is Cardiff on a Six Nations match day. 'It was a phenomenal experience coming to the ground and seeing crowds ten deep outside the coach, Irish and Welsh fans cheering the team,' he said. 'It's a unique thing we have here in the Six Nations. An event like this in Cardiff is a fantastic testament to northern hemisphere rugby.'

Inside the Millennium Stadium press room, I was instructed to 'find some neutrals' for a quick radio chat. Former England internationals turned respectively *Sunday Times* and *Sunday Telegraph* scribes Stuart Barnes and Paul Ackford seemed a good choice. But Barnes's Bassaleg blood coloured his enthusiastic verdict on Welsh chances while Ackford was making mischief marching through the press room shouting: 'Wa-hales, Wa-hales'. With the obvious exception of the Irish media corps, every hack in the room knew a Welsh Grand Slam would be the best story.

After the French, with their usual jammy panache, did just enough to keep themselves in the mix for the championship title, everyone headed for their seats muttering mental arithmetic. A points-difference win would destroy the magic. It had to be Slam, bam, thank you ma'am.

Max Boyce, flanked by Charlotte Church and Katherine Jenkins, lead a deafening rendition of *'Hen Wlad fy Nhadau'*

The fans had obeyed the call to empty their last pub pint and fill the stands in good time. Glanmor's Gap glowed green while the rest of the stadium was a raucous mass of red, responding to the circuiting choir's repertoire of rugby classics. As the Welsh team line-up was announced, the roar that greeted each player's name was immense.

Before the anthems, there were plaudits for special guests and faithful servants. Two of the three Welsh soldiers who were awarded the Military Cross for their actions in Iraq – Fusilier David Evans, 25, of Swansea and Sergeant Neil Griffiths, 30 of Ynysbwl – and a third who was mentioned in dispatches, Sergeant Martin Gregory, 27, of the Rhondda, were given a heroes' welcome on the pitch. Farewells were bid to Wales's most capped player Gareth Llewellyn while choirmaster Hadyn James celebrated his 40th appearance on the podium.

And then came rugby's troubador, guitar in hand, to rev the faithful into a frenzy and 'sing "Hymns and Arias" like you've never sung it before'. We'd never heard these verses before either. Max's retro classic had been re-mastered to fit the occasion. The opening couplets captured the collective mood: '…my nerves are in a state. We haven't had a day like this since 1978,' he sang. '…too close to call. We hope your man O'Driscoll doesn't get the ball at all.'

Max returned to the pitch, flanked by rugby's foxiest anthem songstresses – Charlotte Church and Katherine Jenkins, both in snug-fitting Welsh jerseys with a hint of midriff on show. The big screens remained focused on the trio throughout a deafening rendition of '*Hen Wlad Fy Nhadau*' that could have been heard in Caernarfon. So we never got a reaction shot from Gavin as his then 'firm friend' hit her top *Gwlad*. He must also have spied the naughty banner that was unfurled near the touchline every time Wales scored: 'Henson's Tackle Even Makes Charlotte Wince'.

But it was a storming challenge from Brent Cockbain that made Ireland's golden boy hurt. If the Welsh lock's perfectly legitimate tackle on Brian O'Driscoll summed up the physical intensity of the opening quarter, the Irish captain's retaliation summed up the mental tension. As BO'D riverdanced over Cockbain's back, he was lucky to escape with a ticking-off.

Ireland's strong start jangled Welsh nerves until a clinical Henson drop goal in the 12th minute brightened the mood. Four minutes later Gethin Jenkins eased anxieties further. Charging down Ronan O'Gara's clearance kick, the man they call Melon showed his usual pace and presence of mind to toe it towards the try line. Mike Ruddock joked later that John Toshack was keeping an admiring eye on Jenkins's dribbling skills. And Gethin revealed the score was all the more sweet given O'Gara had sledged him earlier with the sobriquet 'fat bastard.'

A silver-booted 52m special from Henson and another penalty from Stephen Jones built up the points cushion as half-time loomed. During the break, a kick from Cardigan-born Geraint Forster warmed the hearts of the crowd. Geraint, 29, had taken up the Brains/

• •

WRU challenge of Kicking for £50k – even though he hasn't played rugby for 10 years. But the challenge included a spot of pre-match training with Paul Thorburn. Geraint was also determined to do it for a great cause. Having lost close friend Paul Andre Blundell in a rugby accident, he wanted to donate his prize money to the spinal injury charity set up in his memory. Just short at 50m, he whacked it over at 40m, bagging £25,000 and an ovation from 74,000 fans into the bargain. 'Superb!' he beamed.

As the second half opened, Scott Johnson went on cheerleading duty, his hour-glass legs jigging down the touchline. The next 40 minutes had everything: Welsh flair with Shane cheekily gesturing to his back line as if conducting a swing band; fisticuffs from O'Connell and Sidoli and an Irish fightback that caused a few stomach-flipping moments. But the Welsh Grand Slam had already been gift-wrapped in the 57th minute with Kevin Morgan's try, set up by Shanklin off one of the glorious angles he had been running all afternoon. Ruddock's joyful face filled the big screen. The dream was becoming a reality.

Two minutes to go and the entire stadium was on its feet screaming 'Wales, Wales'. One minute to go and the souvenir T-shirts were already being advertised. Full time and Martyn Williams – so appropriate it was him – booted the ball into touch and his team into a new era of Welsh rugby. For that was the most exciting thing about Wales's Grand Slam triumph – March 19, 2005 seemed just the beginning.

*P*ostscript: *Of course we all know what happened next…*

Gethin Jenkins and Stephen Jones
celebrate the opening try of the
Grand Slam decider

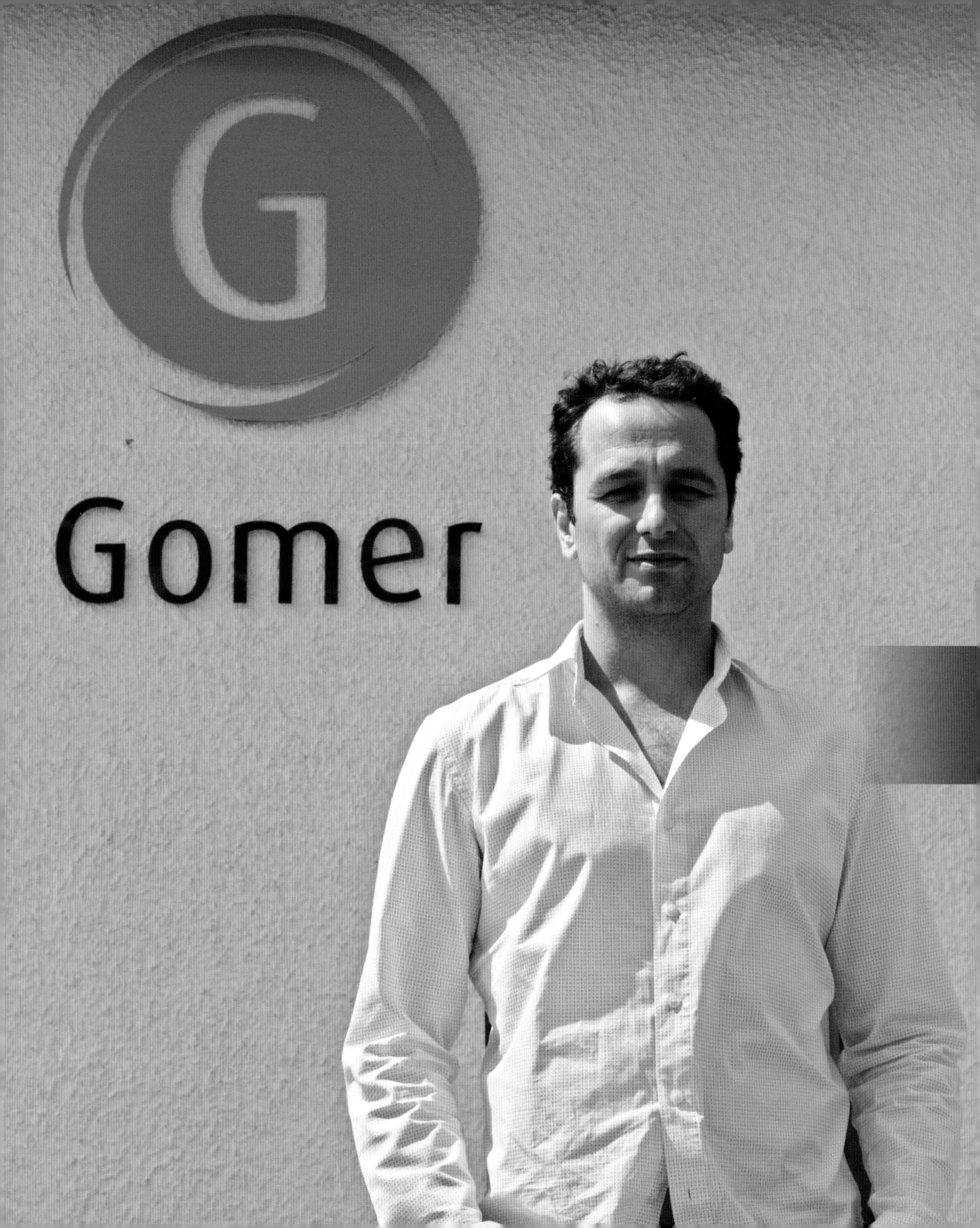
Gomer

Chapter 2

Famous Fans

*I prefer rugby to soccer. I enjoy the violence
in rugby, except when they start biting each
other's ears off.*

Elizabeth Taylor

WALES PLAY IN RED

*W*elsh rugby has never been short of celebrity support. One glimpse of the Three Feathers and even our most stellar names get starstruck. In 2002 I began a series of Celebrity Fan interviews for Wales's match programmes. Sian Phillips was the first. She was appearing on Broadway during that autumn international season but was keeping a keen eye on Wales's progress. When I rang the theatre in New York to arrange the interview, a chap called Percy acted as an extremely enthusiastic go-between. 'It's so lovely to bring two Welsh girls together!' he declared. He rang frequently to ensure I knew the arrangements for the interview, chatting with great charm. 'What a helpful man Percy is,' I told Sian when we finally spoke. 'Don't you know who he is?' she laughed, 'He's Percy Gibson – Joan Collins's husband!'

Sian Phillips

Actress and rugby devotee Sian Phillips *(BBC)*

SIAN Phillips likes her rugby. How could a daughter of Gwauncaegurwen not? The small Swansea Valley town affectionately known as GCG has given us two national icons – the finest actress Wales has produced and its greatest rugby player. And their paths have often crossed over the years.

'Gareth Edwards and I have appeared on various shows together. I knew his mother – a great lady,' she explains. 'I went to interview her when I went back to GCG to do the programme *Down Your Way*. She told me a wonderful story. She slipped on an icy pavement outside her house, hit the ground and passed out. She came to as she was being carried into the house by neighbours. As they put her down in the front parlour, she could hear one saying:

"Is she alright?"

"I don't think so," came the reply. There was a long pause. Then the other one said: "Could have been worse – could have been Gareth!"'

Sian recounts the story of Welshmen getting their priorities right on the phone from New York, where she is appearing on Broadway in Israel Horovitz's dark comedy *My Old Lady*. The eponymous role of a 94-year-old French matriarch who refuses to die, much to the disgruntlement of those around her, is a demanding one. There are six performances a week – two on Saturdays and Sundays. Despite this frenetic schedule, Sian will be tracking Wales's progress in the autumn internationals.

'I'm away so much but I try to keep in touch with how Wales are doing by reading about it and I love to catch an international if I'm in Cardiff. I find rugby terribly exciting – I get

36

· ·

worked up about it. I knew a lot of the stars of Gareth's era. They were so exciting to watch. I'd like to get to know who the stars are now.'

Before Sian shared GCG's pride in Gareth Edwards's success, she was influenced by another local who played a vital role in Welsh rugby history – Eic Davies. The teacher, broadcaster and family friend nurtured her precocious acting talent by persuading her to perform in BBC plays while still a teenager. He pioneered Welsh-language rugby commentary, and he created a mini-dynasty of rugby broadcasters: his son Huw Llewelyn Davies and grandson Rhodri have carried on the family tradition.

'Eic was the Welshest person I'd ever met,' Sian recalls. 'Not just Welsh by accident of birth but passionately Welsh. Our Swansea Valley Welsh was peppered with English words for which there were no Welsh equivalents. Eic challenged us to invent new words to keep up with modern life. He earned a place in Welsh history by translating rugby terms into Welsh, inventing a whole rugby vocabulary so he could broadcast Welsh radio commentaries.'

Eic also renamed his star pupil. Jane Phillips became Sian Phillips – the Welsh version of Jane was hardly used at the time and puzzled people even in Wales. She will never forget her first grown-up billing in a new Welsh play that listed her as Stan Phillips. She was also Eic's sounding board for rugby translation. 'Eic and I would travel all the way from GCG to do broadcasts in Cardiff in his beloved old Austin – you could see light through the bottom of that car – and he would spend the journey trying out terms for rugby commentary, saying 'what do you think of *canolwr* for centre?' And he'd sometimes sneak me into the commentary box for international matches which was very exciting.'

Rugby played its part in her tumultuous 20-year marriage to Peter O'Toole, which she charts powerfully in her autobiography *Public Places*. Like his fellow hell-raising countryman, the late Richard Harris, O'Toole was and is a rugby fanatic. He was delighted to appear in the only advert of his career to promote the 2001 British Lions Tour, morphing from a wizard into a touchline grandad as he booms 'You can!' to a schoolboy player who pulls a rugby ball, Excalibur-like, from the pitch. When O'Toole played schoolboy rugby he split his tongue open and broke his nose – the latter had to be corrected with a spot of plastic surgery before he could film *Lawrence of Arabia*.

'O'Toole was rugby mad,' Sian says. 'We had a great bunch of rugby-loving friends who used to congregate in our house before we went to internationals, including my GP Gerry Slattery.' Dr Slattery used the Irish rugby-medic grapevine when Sian decided to have her second child in Dublin, putting her in touch with his great friend and former player Declan Meagher, who oversaw the birth of her daughter Pat.

'Declan shot across Dublin for the birth and as an ex-Irish rugby international was nonplussed to hear me singing '*Sosban Fach*' while semi-conscious,' Sian remembers. 'He told me later he didn't know whether to pass the baby or score a try!'   *November 9, 2002*

37

Peter O'Toole

*W*hile my rugby conversation with Sian Phillips had been meticulously planned by Joan Collins's husband, a moment of sporting serendipity brought me into contact with her ex-husband on the eve of the 2006 Heineken Cup Final.

Munster fan Peter O'Toole   *(Carolyn Hitt)*

IT was a mirage surely. How else could Lawrence of Arabia be in Cardiff on a rain-lashed Friday night? But the vision was real. Although we had trekked across town from the Welsh Sports Hall of Fame dinner in monsoon conditions desperately searching for a nightcap, this was no fatigue-induced hallucination.

His bright blue eyes gleamed, the cravat was neatly tied and a large brandy swirled in his left hand. Blimey. Peter O'Toole was in the City Arms.

The landlord had already welcomed him with a polite: 'Would you like us to turn the music down, Mr O'Toole?' But as every corner heaved with red-shirted Munster fans, the actor wanted to enjoy the party as much as they did. Mobile phone cameras flashed, hands were proffered for shaking and the thesp charmed everyone who came to pay homage. Like any rugby fan on tour, he just wanted to be one of the boys.

As is appropriate for a legend of stage and screen, he was flanked by security. They were no square-jawed heavies, however. 'These are my beautiful Welsh bodyguards,' he declared by way of introduction. One was my mate Jane, who works in sports PR, the other her equally attractive sister. They had assumed the roles since meeting O'Toole earlier that evening at Cardiff Tennis Club at a quiz organised for rugby journalists here for the Heineken Cup final. The 73-year-old icon, last seen on our screens sharing the role of Casanova with David Tennant, was happy to join the *Western Mail* team. And, according to my colleague Simon Thomas, very useful he was too as they scooped second place.

But would you expect anything less from the rugby-mad actor, who had announced he was in Cardiff as Richard Harris's 'envoy on Earth', ensuring their beloved Munster finally achieved European glory. 'I will never win an Oscar now, but even if I did I would swap it instantly for one sip of champagne from the Heineken Cup,' Harris had written when Munster last appeared in the final. He never lived to see them triumph but this time O'Toole was determined to pop the cork on his behalf.

And here he was in the City Arms. It was too good an opportunity to miss. So many questions to ask of a life lived to the edge and back. I struck up a conversation. O'Toole turned to Jane the Bodyguard. 'Summon the lady in white,' he smiled. 'He says you are now officially Reserve Bodyguard,' Jane informed me as we swapped places.

'*Shwd y' chi?*' O'Toole twinkled. I told him I had hotfooted to the City Arms from the City Hall where, among others, Jack Matthews had been inducted into the Welsh Sports Hall of Fame – the citation given by his former centre partner Bleddyn Williams. 'Ah... Jack and Bleddyn,' O'Toole intoned as if the words were a religious incantation.

He has a particular appreciation of centre play, having spent his own youthful rugby career at number 12. 'So as a centre were you crash-ball or silky?' I asked. O'Toole admitted he was neither when faced with the might of Lewis Jones, the Llanelli and Wales international who was his direct contemporary. He will never forget the sight of Jones thundering towards him when the pair met in a forces match.

His spectating days have been even more incident-filled than his playing experiences. Can you imagine the wondrous hedonism of an international weekend spent with Peter O'Toole, Richard Harris and Richard Burton? His memories of 'Rich' as he called him, were extremely fond. But let's just say he had less time for the Missus, referring to Liz Taylor only as 'That Woman'. Recollections of Stanley Baker were coloured by the Rhondda legend's toughness. 'A hard, hard man,' said O'Toole admiringly.

And then it was his turn to ask questions. When it came to delivering the script of Welsh rugby, O'Toole was word-perfect: 'How's Ryan Jones's shoulder?' he enquired. 'Is Alfie OK? What about Shanklin? And is Gethin Jenkins on form?'

The following day O'Toole turned up in the press box in a fedora hat, a sweeping black coat and a Munster cricket jersey, feeling quietly optimistic. As we queued for the lift to Level 6, he looked at his watch. 'Half an hour to the stage,' he murmured. Inside, 70,000 Munster

Munster's pocket dynamo Peter Stringer helps his team to Heineken Cup glory

• •

fans had already transformed the stadium into pure theatre. I was still on duty as Reserve Bodyguard. O'Toole took my arm and I escorted him to his seat.

The pre-match entertainment unfolded. O'Toole produced his binoculars for the can-can girls, who wiggled their rears in front of a Treorchy Male Voice Choir barely suppressing their delight. Eighty minutes of some of the most raucously-supported rugby the Millennium Stadium has ever witnessed followed.

At half-time, O'Toole turned round. 'What do you think?' he asked tensely. It was close but Munster's hunger for the prize seemed so much more visceral than their French opponents. And how could they fail to be propelled to victory by what coach Declan Kidney later described as the sheer force of 'good will'.

When the thronged streets of Limerick were shown on the big screen and Munster fans on both sides of the Irish Sea enjoyed a moment of intense bonding, for just an instant I rued the day my great-great-grandfather left Cork behind. I thought Welsh supporters knew a bit about passion but anyone who swam in Munster's sea of red for that final will know how special that sporting community is.

The drama continued to the death. Only a boob from giant Fijian wing Bobo, who crashed into his own man as Biarritz mounted one final attack, prevented Munster heartbreak. Utter bedlam erupted as their little bald dynamo and man of the match Peter Stringer hoofed the ball into the stand to signal full time.

O'Toole's blue eyes shone. He squeezed my hand and wrote a message on my match programme: 'For my Reserve Bodyguard, love Peter O'Toole'.

His mission as Richard Harris's earthly envoy was complete. Now his late partner in hell-raising could truly rest in heaven. Neither Cardiff nor Munster would forget that weekend in a hurry. And after meeting Lawrence of Arabia in the City Arms neither will I.

May 22, 2006

Ioan Gruffudd and Matthew Rhys

Having gleaned tales of rugby hedonism from Peter O'Toole about Richard Harris and Richard Burton, it was great to hear their modern-day counterparts share their love of the oval ball.

'I WOULD rather have played for Wales at Cardiff Arms Park than Hamlet at the Old Vic,' Richard Burton once said.

If it wasn't for the slings and arrows of outrageous fortune, Burton just might have got his chance. As a schoolboy, he would have been in line for an international cap had the

Second World War not intervened. In the RAF he played for a representative Welsh side alongside Bleddyn Williams. The Prince of Centres was impressed with the fearless young flanker who would go on to play the Prince of Denmark.

'Mr Williams is kind enough to suggest that I had distinct possibilities as a player were it not for the lure of the tinsel and paint and money and fame and so on,' wrote Burton in his memoirs, adding this was the 'only notice' he cherished. But the actor wrote a more critical review of his own abilities on the rugby stage.

While he conceded he was 'very nippy off the mark' when faced with bigger forwards he felt doomed: 'R. T. Evans of Newport, Wales and the Universe for instance – a racy 14 and a half stone and 6ft 1 and a half inches was a nightmare to play against and shaming to play with, both of which agonies I suffered a lot. Genuine class, of course, doesn't need size though sometimes I forget this.'

So Burton had to be content with showing his genuine class in the theatre rather than the sporting arena but he still allowed the latter to encroach on the former. When a matinee of *Hamlet* coincided with a Welsh international, Shakespeare's tragic hero spent much of the second act straying to the wings where a portable radio crackled with commentary. It was said Gertrude gave Hamlet the final score.

Rugby also featured in his romantic life. Always adept at showing the ladies a good time, he once took Elizabeth Taylor to watch Aberavon RFC. 'I prefer rugby to soccer,' she later commented. 'I enjoy the violence in rugby, except when they start biting each other's ears off.' Sounds like The Wizards made quite an impression on Liz.

Burton's modern counterparts enjoy a similar passion for the game. Tracking Wales's 2005 Grand Slam campaign from a Santa Monica pub overlooking the Pacific Ocean, Ioan Gruffudd felt compelled to leave the Hollywood hills for the green, green grass of home. 'I just had to get back,' he recalled. 'It was awesome. When we beat Scotland I just knew we were going to win the Grand Slam. That's a very rare feeling but there was no doubt we were going to do it. So I booked my ticket and flew home.'

When victory came in the Millennium Stadium that day, Ioan found himself overwhelmed with emotion. 'It was a surreal experience. I don't remember looking into anyone else's eyes. It just felt such a personal moment. It sounds strange but I didn't want to share it with anyone! I just wanted to savour my own feelings.'

Ioan's former school-friend, flatmate and fellow actor Matthew Rhys has also followed Wales from film sets, stages and studios across the world. Like Burton he has combined treading the boards and tuning in to the big game in the wings. When a Royal Shakespeare

Richard Burton – thespian and flanker   *(Western Mail)*

Company production of *Romeo and Juliet* coincided with the Six Nations a few years ago, star-crossed lover Matthew was still able to find out whether it was much ado about nothing or all's well that ends well: 'Thankfully stage managers have radios!'

Since being based in America he rises at the crack of dawn in time for kick-off. 'The Six Nations coincides with the pilot season in Hollywood so the busiest time in LA is when the Six Nations is on. You do find a lot of ex-pats out there. There's one pub in Santa Monica right on the beach which is called the King's Head. It charges you $10 to get in and you get a fried breakfast because kick off for us is 5 or 6 in the morning.

'And that's when you befriend all the Welsh in LA – everyone finds out about the King's Head and turns up for the international. It's quite a bizarre feeling – it's always the valleys boys who are determined to drink at that time of the morning, so they start on the cider! We'll have a pint of Guinness and pack in to this small ex-pat pub by the beach in the early hours of the morning, eating fry-ups and watching rugby.

'It doesn't change – the feelings, the banter and the rivalry. I remember one year, Wales were playing England. Martin Johnson was captaining, sledging at the ref as usual – he was notorious for it. And it was driving us all mad, we all started shouting: 'Oh shut up Johnson!' Until eventually some old English guy turned round and bellowed (*Matthew adopts an exasperated Gielgudesque tone*) 'Will you just shut up!' to all of us. So it doesn't change. I'm by the sea, eating my eggs and bacon with a load of Welsh ex-pats and screaming at a widescreen television.'

But this ardent rugby fan grew up watching his heroes from an even cosier position. 'I can say "I Was There" on a number of occasions in the flesh but more often than not –

Ioan Gruffudd swapped Hollywood for the 2005 Grand Slam decider

when tickets weren't available – I was there in my own living room,' he explains. 'And when it's full of other Welsh supporters it's a sort of terrace in itself really. We felt equally present whether home or at the game in the most glorious moments.'

Just before he returned to Los Angeles for Hollywood's pilot season, Matthew invited me to the living room terrace – his parents' front room – to relive some of those 'glorious moments'. In the States, his profile is higher than ever thanks to his starring role alongside screen sibling Calista Flockhart in the hit series *Brothers and Sisters*. At home in Cardiff in 1993 there was a family drama of a different kind breaking out. As Wales prepared to take on England at the Arms Park it was more a case of *Brother v Sister*.

'I'd like to say I was almost there for Wales's 9–3 victory over England,' Matthew grins. 'There was a whiff of a ticket which never transpired and it was actually my sister who went to the game, which

I was devastated about, especially because of the result we had. It was that phenomenal moment when Ieuan Evans outran, outclassed and outshamed Rory Underwood to produced one of the best sprinting, footballing tries we've seen.

'I remember my sister phoning at the end of the game and she was actually crying because everybody was on such a high. We'd had a few years in the wilderness at that point and Ieuan, on his own, managed to inspire a nation with that beautiful running try. I remember the commentator saying "Underwood just stood still". What was he thinking? He wasn't standing still at all, he was flat out. "How dare you rob Ieuan of the glory!" I thought.

'It was like the chariot race in *Ben Hur*, those two against each other. It just seemed to go on forever. And with that sort of gamble, when he kicks and chases, your senses are so heightened at that moment, you're so euphoric and the run seems to take four-and-a-

Matthew Rhys will never forget watching rugby with Richard Harris *(Gawain Davies)*

half hours because you're so on the edge of your seat. I just saw Ieuan's angle, coming in front of Underwood and thought, "Goodnight Sunshine!" It was fabulous.'

The man, who in Bill McLaren's memorable description, out-magicked Merlin, first caught 14-year-old Matthew's imagination in the living room terrace back in the1988 Five Nations. 'The magnificent jinking Ieuan produced some of the best sidestepping we'd seen since Phil Bennett, when he famously outran many a Scottish defender for a fabulous try. In the same game Jonathan Davies, after Robert Jones had given him a magnificent enormous reverse pass, beautifully grubbered it and then chased with all his little might and walloped it down close to the posts.

'I remember those two instances vividly. It's those moments when you don't shout, you take an enormous intake of breath, moments of absolute inspiration and awe when you realise someone does something almost otherworldly and those were two moments in that game where we all went (*intake of breath*) "Genius!"'

Matthew's own attempts to emulate the men in red came on the playing fields of Ysgol Gyfun Glan Taf, one of Wales's most competitive rugby schools. He played inside centre. So was he a crash-ball type or a weaver of midfield magic? 'I'd like to think I was a silky and imaginative centre – but I played for the second team!'

He didn't harbour acting ambitions until at 16 he was cast as the lead in a school production of *Elvis*. Hooked, he progressed to the Welsh National Youth Theatre and won a scholarship to RADA. His career path since has confirmed his promise as one of the most exciting actors of his generation. He's shared the big screen with Anthony Hopkins in *Titus*, played Benjamin Braddock to Kathleen Turner's Mrs Robinson in the acclaimed West End production of *The Graduate*, and starred as Dylan Thomas, alongside Keira Knightley and Sienna Miller, in *The Edge of Love*, about the poet's romantic entanglements.

And, of course, such profile brings rugby perks. When Wales met England at Wembley in 1999, Matthew didn't have to endure the usual scrabble for tickets with his sister. By the time another legendary victory over the Old Enemy was in the offing, his star had risen sufficiently to ensure one of the best seats in the house.

'I went to Wembley with Ioan Grufudd. Miraculously and very kindly we'd been given hospitality tickets and we found ourselves more or less in the Royal Box! We were sat behind Prince William and his bodyguards. To the left of them were the Manic Street Preachers. We caught their eye and they were smiling as if to say, 'How have we wound up here, what's going on!' We were so grateful to be there – and very apprehensive because of course it was the England game.

'And it was a hell of a game. There was the Scott Gibbs try that came from nowhere – that massive burst. In that moment, it was almost as if he grew horns and a tail because he was like a bull. And reverting back to the beautiful Welsh tradition of jinking, he threw a few blinding sidesteps before crossing the line.

'I remember at the time thinking the space between the try line and the dead-ball line seemed really short. And Gibbs was going at such a pace – he crossed the try line and he was still going. He had the ball in one hand and put the other hand up to the sky, to say "Yes! We've scored a try!" And I remember feeling sheer panic for that split second thinking he's going to cross the dead-ball line and this is going to be worse than Will Carling when he was picked up when he was over the try line.

'And then he puts it down and we just went mental. The feeling was only superseded when Jenkins converted it. We just went nuts. And I remember looking at the Manics and they were just jumping. It was late in the game but we still had to hold on. Everyone was screaming "Watch the drop goal!" but Mike Catt's effort drifted wide. For me Wembley was the defining "I Was There" moment. We hit the pubs and drank them dry that night because it was just glorious.'

But not all Matthew's memorable matches are Welsh. He will never forget a France v Ireland game in Paris – not so much for a classic clash of blue and green but for the colourful company he kept. 'I was in Paris for a film awards ceremony and Richard Harris was to be honoured with a lifetime achievement award. I went into the hotel bar on the Friday night and there he was, sat on his own, no entourage. I couldn't believe it.

'After a few pints I plucked up the courage to go and speak to him. Being the kind of guy he was, he was very happy to chat away and regale me with stories. And then told me that Ireland were playing France the next day. He wasn't going to the match but to a bar to watch it and would I like to join him. To me that invitation was heaven sent! My heroes were

'He puts it down and
we just went mental' –
Matthew Rhys recalls
Scott Gibbs's wondrous
Wembley try

Burton, Harris and O'Toole – all three great rugby fans – so for him to say "Why don't you come to this bar to watch France v Ireland" is certainly a memory I will take to my grave.

'I don't remember much of the match because I was watching Harris watch France v Ireland in Paris. He was only allowed three drinks because the doctor said he should either drink wine or champagne so he had three glasses of champagne while he watched it. But he loved to watch younger men get drunk so he plied and plastered me with French lager as we watched the international. Fabulous!'

As a teenager, Harris played for Munster but had to give up sport after contracting TB. In that Paris bar, the late actor revealed his rugby dream. 'He had this fantasy of hiding in the tunnel wearing the Irish jersey beneath his mac. He wanted to run out with the team and rip off his mac just so he could say he'd worn the green jersey on the turf of Lansdowne Road.' Harris's fellow rugby-mad hell-raiser Richard Burton said he'd forgo all his thespian glories for the chance of playing a single game for Wales. So would Matthew Rhys prefer a cap to an Oscar? 'Running out in the red jersey would be the ultimate – I can't imagine a better rush than scoring a try for Wales.'

February 2009

Huw Edwards

As a good Llanelli boy, Huw Edwards's rugby memories are naturally tinged with scarlet. He also has the essential Stradey Park 'I Was There' moment.

HUW EDWARDS may occupy the hottest seat in BBC news but in 1972 he also had the best seat in Stradey Park – even if he had to bring it with him. 'I was among a group of Llanelli Grammar schoolboys on the touchline when Llanelli beat the All Blacks in that stupendous game,' recalls the ten o'clock news anchorman. 'I was 11-years-old. We paid 5p to see the match and carried gym benches across to Stradey Park to provide extra seating. I still have vivid memories of Delme Thomas being carried shoulder-high after the 9–3 win.'

Like most boys raised in Scarlets territory, rugby played a significant role in Huw's early years. 'I started off in junior school playing on the wing. I was quite a fast runner in those days. And then, when I grew to be among the tallest in the class, switched to the second row and then to wing-forward, or flanker as many now call it. I was never a gifted player, but I did enjoy playing.'

He also enjoyed watching. The Edwards family – father, Hywel, a respected academic, mother, Aerona, a comprehensive schoolteacher, and his younger sister Meinir – were passionate viewers. 'My earliest memories of watching rugby are wet Saturday afternoons at home, with the curtains shut as my dad ranted at the screen. Those were the days when Wales were untouchable and it took a long time for me to get this "guaranteed win" mentality out of my system.'

His English colleagues have helped this process along with the inevitable post-match banter but Huw has his allies in the newsroom. 'Rugby is a regular conversation topic. International matches bring plenty of needle too. But there's a small but solid Welsh contingent here so I don't feel quite as outnumbered as I once did.'

Huw doesn't just play the Welshman on match days. Throughout his career, he has let his roots show. A Cardiff University languages graduate, his broadcasting career began in Swansea Sound as a 'dogsbody on an opera show'. After a BBC traineeship, he joined the BBC Wales newsroom in 1985, and his rise through the journalistic ranks was swift. He moved to BBC News in London as political correspondent in 1988 and went on to cover the downfall of Margaret Thatcher in 1990. He was later appointed chief political correspondent for BBC News 24.

Barely into his 30s, he was asked to read the news for the first time – ten years later he succeeded Peter Sissons in the prime ten o'clock news slot. Thankfully he's ignored advice along the way to ditch his Llanelli lilt. He remembers an

Scarlets fan Huw Edwards   *(BBC)*

● ●

outrageous comment from an experienced colleague, who told him: 'You will do well but you will really have to change that accent. If you have a Midlands or Welsh accent people immediately think you are educationally sub-normal.'

'He was actually being serious,' Huw laughs. 'Anyone who doesn't respect their identity is a bit of a sad person and I'm very proud to be Welsh'.

He's made his home in south London with wife Vicky, a BBC producer, and their four children, but when the Scarlets play he's at Stradey in spirit. 'I support them from a distance. I always make sure I know how they've done. I may be 200 miles away but roots run deep.'

Rugby is not his only sporting passion. And for someone who shares a hometown with Terry Griffiths, the green baize has as much appeal as the Scarlets. 'I like snooker because it is a great leveller. Skiing too, is another favourite of mine. You're testing your own skills, and it's immensely satisfying. I enjoy running, and this again is a great way of pushing your own limits,' he explains.

And when it comes to the choice of Greatest Ever Welsh Player, here is the news from Huw: 'My all time favourite without a shadow of a doubt is Phil Bennett. His qualities: pace, energy, superlative skill, a genius for reading the game and the best side-step ever.'

November 2002

Bill Clinton

In 2001 former US President Bill Clinton came to Wales. I was dispatched to the Hay Festival to get an exclusive 600-word interview. There was just one problem. His bodyguards said I was only allowed to shake his hand. But, as is so often the case, the unifying spirit of rugby came to my rescue...

WHEN it comes to Bill Clinton, David Aaronovitch sums up the presidential paradox perfectly. 'Only Clinton could have got anywhere near a Middle East peace agreement, only Clinton could have left DNA on an intern's cocktail dress.'

My view of Bill tended towards the latter version. I thought he was just a sleazebag with a penchant for bimbos with alarmingly large hair and Arkansas beauty-counter make-up. But that was before I met him. As brief encounters go, it would have blown Celia Johnson off the platform. Within 30 seconds I had completely changed my opinion. Within 60 seconds I was feeling quite envious of bimbos with alarmingly large hair and Arkansas beauty-counter make-up. Meeting Clinton is a quasi-religious experience.

In 2001, he came to the Hay Festival. It was not his first visit to Wales. In 1969, as an Oxford student, he came in search of Dylan Thomas's birthplace. He and a classmate got

Former rugby player Bill Clinton *(BBC)*

as far as Cardiff Central bus station. 'I remember it took forever to get there,' he recalled. 'We got out at the bus station in Cardiff; we stopped at a little pub, there was a Jerry Lewis film on the television – I remember that. We drank a lot of beer and read these poems to each other and I thought they were fabulous.'

The shaggy-haired student reciting 'Do Not Go Gentle' with a southern twang might not have made much impact on the locals in 1969 but his return visit bathed Hay-on-Wye in an international spotlight. Booked to deliver the festival's BBC Wales World Lecture, he appeared for the privileged few at a pre-lecture reception. On the lawns of Cabalva, a small country house in Whitney-on-Wye, it was Merchant Ivory meets *In The Line of Fire*. Welsh *crachach* mingled with London literati, sipping gin cocktails and decked in the festival uniform of crumpled cream linen.

Security was subtle but tight. Granite-faced men in black surveyed the scene in shades and murmured into headsets. And Bill was late, allowing the atmosphere of anticipation to become slightly feverish. The Welsh contingent included billionaire Terry Matthews, plus AMs Mike German, Kirsty Williams, Nick Bourne and Jenny Randerson. On the more stellar side Joseph Fiennes brooded by the champagne table with Alan Rickman, both attracting approving glances from female guests.

Yet by the time the whisper 'He's here!' rippled through the throng, Fiennes and Rickman had all the allure of Cannon and Ball as every female eye focused on the French windows. Attempting to remain nonchalant and form a hurried queue proved a challenge for some as Clinton strode on to the grass, looking thinner and taller than expected.

'Quick, get in line!' whispered television producer Gwenda Griffith, with whom I had been sharing gin cocktails for the past hour. I managed to cheat a bit, squeezing in front of Terry Matthews. The chief of security was polite but adamant, 'Just say hello, shake his hand and move on please.' Stuff that, I thought. Once in a lifetime chance and all that. Emboldened by the gin, I formed three questions in my mind and rehearsed them as the great and the good formed an adoring conga.

Festival director Peter Florence was making the introductions, 'This is Carolyn Hitt, Mr President, one of Wales's leading journalists'. I was so tickled by Peter's flattering foreword I almost froze. But then the Clinton Effect began to take hold. It really is mesmerising, that certain something that political spin-doctors would term spectacularly good interpersonal skills. The rest of us, particularly the females of the species, recognise it as the charm of the seducer. The handshake is rock-solid while not even your optician gives you this much direct eye contact. But above all there's the impression he gives – for a few moments at least – that the gibberish you're spouting is the most scintillating conversation he has ever heard.

Hands gripped, eyes locked, megawatt smiles broadened, 'How are you enjoying Wales, Mr Clinton?'

'It's wonderful, thank you.'

'So Chelsea's going to Oxford then?'

'Yes, Univ college.'

We needed to move our chat away from the realms of one-liners so I resorted to an age-old strategy for developing male-female interaction. When in doubt, talk sport.

'I hear you were quite a rugby player when you were at Oxford,' I asked with, I am ashamed to admit, a slightly coquettish tilt of the head.

Bingo! Best button to press. He was away, enthusiastically recalling his love of the game.

'I played for my college – I was a flanker.'

Flanker? Oh. My. God. Bill Clinton had just told me he was a flanker. I could dine out on that line for the rest of my life.

'I was one of the biggest guys in the team – but now I'd be one of the smallest.'

The rugby chat was flowing. He remembered his first try, thinking of it as a 'touchdown'. There was the 'strange formation' of the scrum, such an alien concept to an American footballer. Then the match he played through with a minor concussion and the instruction from the coach to just get back on the field 'and get in someone's way.'

It was just me, Bill and rugby. But at this point, the 100 or so crumpled creams in the queue for their presidential audience were practically riverdancing with impatience. The chief of security had also placed a warning hand in the small of my back and gave me a gentle shove. Not wanting to risk Death by Linen – or armed security guard – I reluctantly ended our tactics talk and moved on, beaming inanely across the lawn to compare notes with other survivors of the Clinton Effect. 'How was it for you?' I asked Mike German. 'Well, the earth didn't move,' he replied dryly. Jenny Randerson, looking positively aglow, begged to differ. 'He was really clued up on devolution, and particularly impressed by the number of women we have in the Assembly.'

At the post-lecture gala banquet, Clinton met his match in the charm offensive stakes as Cerys Matthews took the stage. Matching his gaze, Cerys's breathy Pembrokeshire tones floated across the tables. 'We want to change the constitution so you can still be President,' she purred like a modern Monroe, before launching into a duet with Eliza Carthy. Accompanied by a single fiddle, the pair sang '*Lisa Lân*' and an old Civil War song 'How Can I Keep From Singing'. How Can I Keep From Looking was written on Clinton's face.

And while Mick Jagger told me never to name-drop, how can I keep from telling the story of the time I talked rugby with Bill Clinton.

The moment Bill told me he was a flanker *(Carolyn Hitt)*

WALES
PLAY IN RED

Chapter 3

Me and Max Down Under:
The Rugby World Cup 2003

I Was There.
Max Boyce

And so was I.
Carolyn Hitt

....

I've worked with Max Boyce as a producer for many years and in 2003 we travelled to the Rugby World Cup together with our cameraman-come-sound engineer Terry Lewis to record Max Down Under, a series of radio programmes and video diaries for BBC Wales. He would also perform a sell-out televised concert at Sydney Opera House – supported by a then relatively unknown Katherine Jenkins. I'd seen her perform for the first time at the farewell party for the Welsh team and asked her afterwards if she fancied singing in Sydney Opera House.

It was a fantastic adventure and, buoyed by the way Wales lit up the tournament, I ended up staying longer than planned. From the minute we touched down in Australia, the pace was non-stop.

Down Under and Up and Running

Wednesday October 8

After a 22-hour journey we make our bleary-eyed entry into Sydney Airport at 5am.

'Can you say that place with the long name, mate?' asks the Aussie Customs man, as Max approaches with his guitar case. Max's flawless recitation of Llanfair PG and one verse of the national anthem ensures he doesn't even have to put his luggage through the X-ray machine.

John Alwyn Jones, our ex-pat fixer, is on the phone within five minutes of arriving at the hotel. Would we like to view the Lighting the Harbour Bridge ceremony from the Opera House that night and watch the Australian and Argentine teams receive their caps? As dusk falls, it's pure glamour on the harbour front. A media scrum and Sydney's movers and shakers mingle on the forecourt of the Opera House. Gleaming with health, the players file onto two platforms in their best suits as Aboriginal dancers perform a slightly eerie welcome on their didgeridoos.

Max meets Bob Carr, the Premier of New South Wales and International Rugby Board chairman Syd Millar and the Australian Rugby Union chief executive John O'Neill come to say hello. Irish and Welsh referees, David McHugh and Nigel Whitehouse, respectively, ask for 10 tickets for his Opera House concert. 'All the refs want to come,' adds McHugh.

The night ends in an extravaganza of pyrotechnics as a giant golden rugby ball glows on the Harbour Bridge. We get the feeling Australia are going to be rather good at hosting the world cup.

• •

Thursday October 9

7am: A frenetic day of promotional interviews begins at Sunrise, the network television breakfast show hosted by Melissa and David. ABC radio's glamorous rugby buff Sally Loane asks about the linguistic origins of 'Oggi, Oggi, Oggi' while Daniel Lewis from the *Sydney Herald* demands to know why Welsh rugby is so dire. It turns out his mother is from Gorseinon.

On the Opera House steps, Channel 10 News ask Max for his views on 'Matildagate'. The IRB's refusal to allow Australia its unofficial anthem before the games has incensed the country. The lyrics are being printed on the back of rail tickets to the stadium while one DJ has mixed a record of 600 listeners calling in to sing a verse and is playing it round the clock.

Two more radio interviews and an item with Fox Sports Television round off the publicity schedule. We end the day in Sydney's Chinatown in a restaurant that has more squirming sea-life in the foyer than *The Blue Planet*. Very late night with S4C's world cup crew. Max impresses Gerald Davies with his in-depth knowledge of unoaked chardonnay. Gerald deadpans that his 'father would often open up a bottle of unoaked chardonnay when he came up from the mine in Llansaint.'

Friday October 10

8am: Arrive at Sydney Harbour to climb the bridge and record a spectacular trail for Max's Opera House concert.

8.10am: Leave Sydney Harbour because we've all failed the pre-climb breathalyser. Drop in on David Campese instead in his sports shop on The Rocks.

He's hosting a party of young cancer sufferers, making sure each one is kitted out with autographed Wallaby kit and goodies. The walls are lined with photos of Campo's greatest moments and his one famed disaster – a framed print of Ieuan Evans intercepting his pass on the try line to score and give the British Lions the series against Australia is prominently displayed. 'This is Max Boyce, kids, one of the most famous comedians in the world,' he announces. Max replies, 'Ieuan Evans should open a shop like this in Llanelli.'

12noon: Max is the guest speaker at the Heineken Rugby World Cup Luncheon at Sydney's swish Westin Hotel. It's a tough audience of 600 Aussie corporate types but by the end of their lunch they're on their feet, led by Max in an alternative performance of the All Blacks' haka to the rhythm of 'Humpty Dumpty'. I am astounded by Max's stamina. Still feeling the effects of the unoaked chardonnay, Terry and I can barely lift our heads off the table.

4pm: Pass the Bridge Climb breathalyser and ascend the huge iron structure to see arguably the most famous view in the world from the best possible angle.

. . . .

Turn down three tickets to the opening ceremony and match because we have to edit through the night but catch the awesome festivities on TV – how on earth did they create the 'animated' rugby player formed from hundreds of colour-coded schoolchildren?

Saturday October 11

Arrive in a brisk Melbourne – Australia is having its worst spring weather for years. In the taxi we remark on the lack of fat people Down Under. Almost everyone is svelte and healthy. Then a large belly hoves into view. It belongs to a Welsh fan.

Get to hotel and catch up with the papers. Everyone is tipping New Zealand to win the tournament rather than England. The thought of according the Poms favourites' status is even more unpalatable to an Aussie than a Welshman.

Sunday October 12

Head to the Telstra Dome for Wales's opening match. Expats everywhere, parents with Welsh accents shepherd youngsters with broad Aussie twangs and red jerseys towards the turnstiles.

Max gets mobbed every two minutes. Terry the cameraman warns, 'We're running out of tape', but miraculously produces some more to film 'Chicks on Tour', a group of Canadian lovelies with Maple leaves on their cheeks. Inside the stadium, we're so far from the pitch, only Duncan Jones's flaxen curls are visible.

But that's Aussie Rules venues for you. Wales's jittery start gives way to a try fest. The Welsh fans are sufficiently relaxed to turn to Max and give at least six renditions of 'Oggi, Oggi, Oggi'. A lone Wallaby who converts it to 'Aussie, Aussie, Aussie' is cheerily booed.

We bump into Chris Wyatt on the way home, who tells us the boys are feeling good.

It's my birthday and Max produces a bottle of unoaked chardonnay. But I'm so jetlagged I fall asleep nose-down on my editing clip-board.

Canberra...like Cwmbran without the Glamour

Monday October 13

Arrive in Canberra, the Australian capital and our base for the next fortnight. Sense this isn't going to be the most exciting place in the Southern Hemisphere when the taxi driver includes the Truckers' Association Headquarters on his list of notable buildings. The city is apparently known for the 'Three Ps – Politics, Pyrotechnics and Porn.' We see plenty of evidence of the first P. There are government departments and embassies on ever corner. No evidence of the second, but it's so quiet that loud bangs could be a serious threat to health and safety.

And the only hint of the third is a large advert in the hotel directory of services for the Adult World Superstore in Wollongong Street, which appears to be an out-of-town Toys'R'Us with a difference. The customer endorsements suggest Canberrians have a rather matter-of-fact approach to the purchase of sex products: 'We use Adult World's price guarantee all the time and we save heaps!'

Tuesday October 14

A full day's filming in this surreal city. Artificially created as the Australian seat of government when Sydney and Melbourne couldn't agree on capital status, it feels like a film set – *Invasion of the Body Snatchers* meets *The Stepford Wives*. Our hotel, meanwhile, is like *The Shining*, only quieter and without a raving psychopath on the loose. Our fellow guests, the Tongan team, spend a lot of time looking bored rigid in reception. Canberra is very green – 300 trees for every resident – and a symmetrical swirl of roads built around its giant man-made lake add to the sense of feeling part of a 1970s science fiction movie. We expect to see Michael York and Jenny Agutter making a Logan's Run for it any minute. On the plus side, the locals are extremely friendly and used to defending Canberra's honour as a low-crime, peaceful and welcoming city.

First stop Parliament House. Its accessibility is astounding. There are school parties down every corridor and just days before George Bush arrives, we are left to our own devices on the roof to film. Before arriving at the Australian War Memorial, the country's most popular tourist attraction, I get a call from its publicity officer Laura Ryan. 'Would you mind if I brought my Nanna and Grandad along,' she asks, after running through possible filming locations, 'They're Welsh and they'd love to meet Max.' After touring the memorial, a brilliantly devised museum exploring Australia's war history, we sit down with Laura and her grandparents Jim and Gwyneth Gregory. Jim – who used to be called Emrys but the Aussies couldn't pronounce that – brought his family from the Rhondda to Australia in 1955. 'We had two Pommie kids and then had two Aussie kids,' he laughs, Wattstown accent still perfectly intact. Second generation Laura is proud of her Welsh heritage: 'My mum was born in Llwynypia, she's been trying to teach me the words of the national anthem all my life. There are 11 of us going to watch Wales here and we'll be in red from top to toe.' Jim then unrolls three posters he has kept since Max first toured Australia in 1978 and asks him to sign the pictures of Max looking about 15 with more hair than the Jackson Five combined.

Wednesday October 15

A day spent confined to the hotel room with a very temperamental laptop, editing and crashing in rotation. At one point it looks as if we've lost an entire programme. I never knew it was possible to feel such malice towards a lump of circuit boards. Film some short pieces in the hotel bar. In an effort to make it look less like the Marie Celeste I grab a group of tipsy conference delegates from the Australian Protection Services and persuade them to be the backdrop. 'No worries,' says one, 'I've got a good Welsh name – Bryn Meredith.' 'There's a very famous Welsh rugby player called Bryn Meredith,' I tell him. 'I know,' he grins, 'He's my great uncle.'

Thursday October 16

Queue up alongside HTV Wales to satellite programme back from a TV station in a field outside Canberra. The Aussie techies are so laid back, there should be hammocks at their desks. I am less relaxed when the satellite link drops mid-transmission. At one point, Terry the cameraman is flat on his stomach, feverishly plugging leads into any available port, the Aussie techie is unravelling 40ft cables and I'm on two mobile phones, one to Cardiff and one to someone in London who is talking to someone in New Zealand about why a link that routes from Canberra, via Melbourne, London, Bristol and Llandaff, has disappeared. Two

Former Wales fitness coach Andrew Hore and wing Mark Jones relaxing after the RWC 2003 quarter finals *(Carolyn Hitt)*

hours and one re-organised satellite link later, we are having a late night supper when half the Welsh team burst in and pay homage to Max. Fitness coach and chaperone Andrew Hore explains the boys who are not involved with Sunday's match are being allowed a night of supervised socialising. Spirits are high and Brent Cockbain's Welsh language singing repertoire is growing by the day. The Aussie-Welshman is also the Jamie Oliver of the tour, famed for his ability to rustle up team meals from scratch. And we are told that Max must hear Gareth Cooper's impressions of him.

Friday October 17

The Demon Laptop strikes again, wiping out half a radio programme just before it's due to be sent home. We are sending it via the internet. This morning, however, the front page lead on *The Australian* newspaper is the scandal of Australia's 'snail-mail' internet. In a suburban business centre, a process that usually takes 20 minutes is going to take two hours – and its married managers Arthur and Marilyn should have shut up shop half an hour ago. 'Don't worry,' says Arthur, 'We'll leave you here and you can lock up after you.' 'Are you sure you trust us?' I ask. 'Of course,' says Marilyn. 'I was born in Swansea and moved here when I was five – my father went to school with Harry Secombe.'

Saturday October 18

Downtown Canberra is beginning to fill up with Welsh fans, congregating in the Irish pub of choice, King O'Malleys. Max is mobbed by three boys from Merthyr. 'Oi Max! Can we have a photo with you?' The trio then realise they haven't got a camera. 'Hang on Max, we'll go and buy one!' And they did. After a week of one-sided minnow-crushing contests – apart from Fiji v USA – the Rugby World Cup finally comes alive with the England v South Africa match. England are spectacularly unpopular with the Aussie press, who have spent days dissecting the legality of Neil Back's rolling maul tactics in tedious detail. Settle in the bar to watch the 10pm kick-off game, not really knowing who to support. After Will Greenwood's pivotal try, it looks as if the only thing England are going to lose in the next couple of weeks are those fancy lycra shirts.

Sunday October 19

Torrential rain can't dampen the spirits of the Welsh fans gathered in Murphy's Shooters Bar, a less than salubrious watering hole in the centre of Canberra. Matthew Davies from Trimsaran leads the singing. He doesn't just know all the words to Max's songs – he can recite the chat in between from *Live At Treorchy*.

At the stadium, which is normally home to the ACT Brumbies, the sizeable Welsh contingent are in good voice. Most of the neutrals shout for Tonga, and to be fair to the Friendly Islanders, they provide more to shout about. Their efforts may be ridden with mistakes but at least they have some fire in their bellies. Wales, by contrast, look lacklustre and directionless. Thank the lord – as usual – for Martyn Williams, who turns the game with a surprise drop goal and try. At the final whistle, the Tongans thank the crowd for their support by performing a touchline haka, while their coach Jim Love says Italy were far more aggressive than Wales and reveals the preparation that has gone into their world cup campaign: 'We're on a nil budget and have been together for three weeks.'

Steve Hansen rates the Welsh performance as 5 out of 10, 'but at least we won'. It is left to his predecessor, sitting quietly at the back of the press conference, to sum up exactly what was missing from Wales's second world cup match. Graham Henry turns to Max, with that sardonic smile we used to know so well, and says: 'There was no-one out there tonight to grab the game by the short and curlies.'

Soundman Terry captures Max's interview with Jean the Faggots Lady in Sydney
(Carolyn Hitt)

• •

Light relief on the way home is provided by Jean Richards, who emigrated from Llanelli in 1970. Dressed in full Welsh costume, she tells Max she will be three rows from the front in his Sydney Opera House Concert next week, with a tray of warm Welsh faggots. In 1978, she turned up at the Welsh team hotel, similarly attired and gave Clive Rowlands a tray of her culinary treats for the team. They lost to Australia the next day. Jean has been wondering whether it was the faggots ever since.

World Leaders Arrive

Monday October 20

There are three presidents in town this week: George W. Bush (United States), Hu Jintao (China) and Max Boyce (Glynneath RFC). The citizens of Canberra are kept awake by the circling of Bush's security helicopters, whilst in the Rydges Capital Hill Hotel, we get the added lullaby of Max's late-night singing with the Tongan team. As he flies to Melbourne for a day of publicity interviews, I head into the centre of Canberra for some retail therapy. Its main department store is called Grace Brothers, but sadly there's no sign of Mrs Slocombe. Max returns late evening having bumped into some old friends in Melbourne. David Attenborough was also on the publicity interview circuit. And England captain Martin Johnson and his team-mate Josh Lewsey say hello in the street. Josh greets Max in Welsh – his mother is from Ystalyfera – and tells him his parents are trying to get tickets for the Sydney Opera House concert.

Tuesday October 21

Lunch at the National Press Club of Australia, where the Telstra Address, a monthly televised speech, is taking place. Photographs of past speakers line the walls, including Bishop Desmond Tutu and Bill Gates. Today it's the turn of two sons of Wales: Swansea-born Aneurin Hughes, former European Union Ambassador to Australia and Canberra's Rugby World Cup Ambassador, and Gerald Davies. The audience of Aussie movers and shakers lap up the tale of Aneurin's Uncle Islwyn, who played for Wales in the 1920s while the politicians warm to Gerald's anecdote about Nye Bevan, complete with stammer impression. The organisers try to persuade Max to return on Friday and share the stage with former Wallaby coach Rod McQueen.

We spend the evening watching the game in the bar, hoping Canada will do us a favour by beating Italy. Max's support for the Canucks is so vocal, a Canadian assumes he is a fellow native.

'Where are you from?' he asks.

58

'Ottawa,' Max deadpans.

'I'm from Ottawa!' says the delighted fan, 'Which part?'

'Er…south side,' Max mumbles.

'Me too! Where exactly?'

'Richmond,' Max improvises.

'Don't know it,' says the bemused Canadian.

Wednesday October 22

Team press conference in the sunshine at the West Rugby Club outside the city. Australian rugby clubs seem a world away from Welsh ones, a cross between leisure complexes and family pubs. And they all have 'pokies', lines of fruit machines, which, rather controversially, help fund youth rugby. Max asks Iestyn Harris whether he's suffering from 'cabin fever' but the centre says he and room-mate Martyn Williams get on fine, especially as the latter does all the cooking. We request a special interview with scrum half Gareth Cooper, having been told he is the choirmaster of the team. His repertoire includes rugby club staple 'Running Bear' and 'Hymns and Arias'. Max asks him for royalties. Steve Hansen asks if the team can have a video of Max's Sydney Opera House concert as they will still be in Canberra when it is staged.

Thursday October 23

George W. Bush's 21-hour flying visit begins, or as our cabbie driver says, 'The despot's in town, mate.' Dubya reveals he played rugby but wasn't very good at it (there's a surprise) as John Eales presents him with a Wallaby-USA jersey. Thousands of anti-war demonstrators gather at Parliament House. Our cameraman Terry is tempted to join the march until he learns it begins at 9am. He is not an early-rising radical. We edit this week's radio programme, chuckling through an entire minidisc of young Welsh fans giving Max a hero's welcome at the Gwlad Website Welsh Supporters' Party. A meal in one of Canberra's swankier eateries is organised by *The Times* sportswriter John Hopkins. Robert Jones and his Radio 5 Live team join us around the table. A lively debate ensues when Radio 5's Ian Carter describes the prospect of losing this Saturday's game as 'oblivion for Wales'. Mark Reason of the *Daily Telegraph* takes issue with the term 'oblivion', arguing that it wouldn't surprise anyone if Wales failed to qualify. It would feel like oblivion to me.

Friday October 24

Max's concert is officially a sell-out, so much so that the Opera House staff have opened up an area of seating usually held in reserve. Great news. It also means I have a definite answer for the callers begging for tickets around the clock. Our hotel is finally dragged out of its

Colin Charvis on the charge against Italy as
Wales make their way to the quarter-finals

corporate slumber with the welcome arrival of Ray Gravell and 60 Welsh fans. Grav is his usual ebullient self, although he is concerned that his eight-year-old daughter's little pink case is arriving on a later plane. 'She has to have it. She's distraught – her Scarlets jersey is in there!' Suffering from pre-match tension, I have an early night in with the telly. Now realise why Australia is such an impressive sporting nation. Its television is abysmal. This must be why everyone spends so much time outdoors doing something less boring instead. Also amazed by how little British news leaks through. This week is an embarrassing exception, however, as a racist North Wales policeman makes the international headlines.

Saturday October 25

Two pre-match functions to attend – lunch at the Canberra Royals Rugby Club with the more sedate travelling Welsh fans, and beers in Murphy's Shooters Bar in the city centre with the young backpacking Taffs. At the former, my attempts to wire up Grav's personal microphone while kneeling behind his podium prompts some typical Aussie innuendo from the former Wallaby MC. At the latter, its utter bedlam as word has spread that Max is in the Building. Feeling seriously nervous about the next 80 minutes, we take our seats in the open-air stand and are almost propelled on to the pitch by the decibel level of the pensioner blasting the national anthem behind us. The old chap apologises in a Gog-Aussie twang. Since leaving Porthmadog 60 years ago he doesn't get much chance to sing in Welsh. Max thrashes around anxiously in his seat, arms flailing as Wales proceed to kick, kick and kick again. At the final whistle, I feel as if I've sustained those 174 tackles, or at least 89 elbowings. 'Thank God for that,' says Max, overwhelmed with relief. 'Bring on the English!' chirp Ponty Boys On Tour in the row behind. Twelve thousand miles away, my mother finally emerges from the kitchen after being unable to stand the tension of watching the match. We discuss the quarter final on a crackly mobile and with the optimism unique to the Welsh rugby fan she utters the immortal catchphrase: 'Well you never know…'

Sunday October 26

Time to leave Canberra as the clocks go forward in Australia and back in Wales. Feel strangely attached to its surreal environs after 13 nights. We discuss Wales's huge defensive performance with a couple on our flight to Sydney. 'Before you say anything, I'd better warn you I'm Adam Jones's mother,' laughs the wife. I tell her I'm a big fan of the Hair Bear Bunch Front Row. 'Those curls are completely natural!' she says. As the small propeller plane circles Sydney Harbour, Max points at the world's most iconic building and still can't quite believe that in 24 hours he'll be inside it in front of 2,500 people. Three presidents came to Australia this week – but only one sold out the Opera House.

Rocking the Opera House and rattling New Zealand

Monday October 27

The day of the Sydney Opera House concert. Max, Terry the cameraman and I have lunch in our favourite café – The Naughty Chef Noodle Bar, all you can eat for $10. Max is pensive over his chilli beef, silently running through his act. The quiet preparation continues in the cab to the stage door. 'This feels like the Green Mile,' he murmurs. The Hungarian taxi driver insists on filling the conversational gaps. 'So you big famous English person like Sir Elton John?' he booms.

'Not quite. And I'm Welsh.'

'But Welsh part of United Kingdom, same thing, no? Are you like Sir Mick Jagger or Sir Paul McCartney?'

'Separate language, separate country and no I'm not like Sir Mick Jagger or Sir Paul McCartney'.

'Sir Roger Moore James Bond?'

To satisfy the Hungarian's curious obsession with knighted celebrities and clear up the differences between Wales and England we tell him Max is like Sir Anthony Hopkins – but with jokes and songs. 'Aaaaaaah!' says the cabbie knowingly, 'Dame Shirley Bassey Welsh!'

As Max rehearses, we interview his support acts, The Australian Girls Choir and soprano Katherine Jenkins. Aged between 11 and 18, the choristers are mini celebrities down under, having performed at the Sydney Olympics and provided the theme tune for Quantas. All eyes, dazzling smiles and immaculately delivered soundbites, only one question floors them. 'Er no… we haven't learned Oggi, Oggi, Oggi,' says bemused section leader Theresa as the room is filled with teenage giggles.

Half an hour before the concert begins we pop our head around Max's dressing room, a huge space with a Steinway grand piano and view of the Harbour Bridge. He is sitting quietly on the settee. 'Good luck!' we whisper, thumbs aloft. Downstairs, two-and-a-half thousand people are streaming through the foyer, including Graham and Raewyn Henry; David Campese; former England winger David Duckham; 21 world cup referees carrying yellow cards and Jean the Faggots Lady in full Welsh costume. 'We're really looking forward to it,' says Graham Henry, 'Max was great to us when we were in Wales.' David Campese, who first sampled Boycean humour at a sevens tournament in Dubai in 1985, is a little disturbed that 'a lady in full Welsh costume' has been prodding him in the back excitedly. Looks like Jean the Faggots Lady has made a new friend.

Catching up with Raewyn and Graham Henry in Sydney Opera House

(Carolyn Hitt)

8.00pm: Draped in banners and dragons, the auditorium is reaching fever pitch. Max runs onto the stage hoisting a huge Welsh flag as if roaring into battle. The Opera House resounds to 2,500 people singing 'Waltzing Matilda'. And I relax, bellowing the counterpoint to the opening 'Oggi, Oggi, Oggi' along with everyone else. It's going to be a huge success.

Asking world cup referees if they need a fourth official
(Carolyn Hitt)

Tuesday October 28

The morning after. That last chardonnay with the referees seemed a good idea at the time – by the fifth glass I was telling David McHugh, Nigel Williams and Alan Lewis I could be their fourth official. Should have soaked up the alcohol with some of the delicacies left at the hotel by Jean the Faggots Lady. But no time to sleep off the hangover. We have to can another link with Max on the steps of the Opera House before he flies off to Adelaide and Melbourne for more concerts. A day of editing rounded off with a trip across the Harbour for a fish supper at the legendary Doyle's restaurant. In the water taxi, the phone rings. 'You won't know me from a bar of soap, love,' says an Aussie voice, 'but my husband Kevin's mother Nancy knew your mother June, and your parents' neighbour Terry said you were in Sydney so we thought we'd just say hello and you're welcome to come out to Manly and see us'. Fair play. The New South Wales Branch of the Llwynypia Mafia are very active.

Wednesday October 29

The *Sydney Morning Herald* carries an enthusiastic review of the concert, gleefully repeating Max's Canberra jokes verbatim, including 'I looked at my watch. It was ten to nine in Sydney… it was 1958 in Canberra.' A Canberra rugby PR chief, who wasn't at the concert but has read the paper, doesn't see the funny side. He screams so loudly down my mobile that that I have to hold it six inches from my ear as he informs me the 'people of Canberra are filthy this morning!' 'Filthy' apparently means a bit cross and has nothing to do with the fact that the city is the porn capital of Australia. I explain that there were also jokes about Sydney, Melbourne and Adelaide, and a Sydney journalist would naturally highlight the Canberra gags but he carries on at a volume that could be heard in Tasmania. 'I've been to Cardiff once and that wasn't a very nice city,' he fumes, expecting me to feel Anne Robinson-ed. He obviously doesn't know that Wales is everybody else's Canberra.

Thursday October 30

Max is in concert in Melbourne. We're in our hotel rooms editing in Sydney. Performing at the city's vast entertainment complex, the Crown Casino, he asks them to shut the bar while

....

he's on stage. 'No worries,' they say, 'Tom Jones asked for the same.' After a day hunched over the lap-top I take a late-night walk in Chinatown and have a Seated Thai Massage on the pavement. It hurts like hell.

Friday October 31

A night on the town stretches into the early hours. Max meets old pals Stan 'The Pies' Thomas and his brother Peter in the Hyatt Hotel. There's also someone who is only referred to as Three Lungs, a nickname celebrating his legendary stamina when he played for Cardiff in the 1970s. I play 'Hymns and Arias' on the hotel piano as Max improvises a new verse about the *Western Mail*. Then he informs Terry the cameraman and me that we are 'going on a pilgrimage'. At 1.30am we're in King's Cross, Sydney's cheerful red-light district. Max stayed here during his first tour of Australia in 1978. 'Does this mean we're going to the Pink Pussy?' I ask, somewhat warily. We have been promised a visit to this dubious establishment for the past six months. It no longer exists… if it ever did in the first place. The fountain that Max once jumped into, head first 25 years ago, is still there, however. Terry is keen for a repeat performance from all three of us, but I manage to dissuade him, a feat that is replicated on the steps of The Stripperama Club five minutes later. 'Come in love, you'll enjoy it more than those two – it's mixed!' growls the doorman. I give him my primmest 'no thank-you.' At 4.30am it's finally stop-tap in a bar that's a real home from home, i.e. it feels just like a Merthyr lock-in.

Saturday November 1

At last. Some sightseeing in Sydney. We go our separate ways to watch Ireland cruelly defeated by Australia. In Darling Harbour's fashionable Cargo Bar there are lots of familiar faces in front of its giant outdoor screen, including HTV sports presenter Rhodri Davies, former Wales fly half Gareth Davies and the entire Radio Wales team. Across town, Max is keeping First Minister Rhodri Morgan entertained at Sydney Rugby Club.

Sunday November 2

Ever since the Sydney Harbour Bridge Climb it's been a running joke that Terry and I failed to have our picture taken at the top while Max has been reminding us of his souvenir photograph on a daily basis. We wreak revenge by having ourselves superimposed into the Welsh line-out on a giant poster, snatching the ball from a Wallaby lock. Just one of the day's displacement activities to take our minds off the expected annihilation by New Zealand at 8.30pm. In the cab to the stadium, 59–10 is the predicted scoreline, until Max's pianist Dick points out that would mean Wales scoring a try. But Wales have other ideas, turning the next 80 minutes into the most exhilarating match of the world cup. Didn't we always know

64

Jonathan Thomas was one of the stand out players when Wales gave the All Blacks a scare

that given half a chance Shane Williams would light up the field for Wales like an exploding little firecracker? While Jonathan Thomas's immense performance showed just why the team management have earmarked him as a future captain. At half-time our section of the crowd is in delirium. By the time Wales take the lead, heads are shaking with ecstatic disbelief throughout the stadium. Max is dancing, I've lost my voice and Terry has a grin as wide as Sydney Harbour. Of course, it couldn't last. Yet Max sums up the mood of the fans when he says, 'I've never felt so euphoric after losing'. But just imagine if we'd won. And next Sunday, just imagine if…I'd better stop now. Brisbane here we come.

A Heroic End to Wales's World Cup Dreams

Monday November 3

Wake up with sore head, no voice and a big smile. But was it all a dream? No. The *Sydney Herald* confirms that last night we almost stitched up the not-so-mighty All Blacks. 'We imagined they would be Red Pussycats, not Dragons,' writes one disgruntled Kiwi. Purring over my flat white latte – coffee lingo is very different down under – I switch to the horoscopes. Jonathan Cainer is instructing Librans throughout the Southern Hemisphere to 'Act on impulse not intellect.'

• •

So I did.

'G-day ma'am. You're through to Qantas Reservations. This is Kim speaking. How may I help?'

'I'm supposed to be flying home on November 10 after the Rugby World Cup quarter finals but my team did so well I want to fly home after the semis in case they beat England and keep going.'

Kim lost her measured phone voice.

'Wales you mean? Too right. Good on ya. We were barracking for them last night. They were awesome. My dad's Welsh.'

Shell out for a Sydney hotel room at triple the usual rate, not to mention $300 for a semi-final ticket. There's nothing like the eternal optimism of the Welsh fan. The news from home is that the viewing figures for *Max Boyce Down Under* were fantastic. As it's our last night together before Max leaves, the three of us celebrate in a BYO Vietnamese restaurant, bringing our own Australian bubbly to wash down the satay chicken. Max is renowned for his culinary sense of adventure – he swears blind he once ordered an entire frog in aspic. Tonight is no exception as he plumps for the mystery dessert 'Icy Salty Plum'. But there is no mystery. A glass arrives full of ice, salty water and a rather tired plum. Terry takes one sip and almost regurgitates his coffee ice-cream. A 'nightcap' at a local 24-hour bar, turns into early morning drinks. Pack for Brisbane at 5am

Thankfully the Welsh team resisted Max's suggestion to respond to New Zealand's war dance with the Humpty Dumpty Haka

Tuesday November 4

Farewell to Max and hello Brisbane. The weather and the welcome are equally warm. Almost every local I encounter strikes up a conversation. A question keeps recurring. 'Did you win today?' 'Er no. We're not playing until Sunday.' It is only when I stumble into what appears to be a giant wedding reception at the hotel that the penny drops. It is Melbourne Cup Day. All Australia is on the razz for its biggest day at the races. The event may take place in Melbourne but it doesn't stop the population of Brisbane – and every other Australian city – donning formal wear and partying into the night. Not for the first time on this trip, I reflect that the whole of Australian culture revolves around sport… or maybe just betting on it.

Wednesday November 5

After several encounters in the lift with very large men, the terrifying truth emerges. We are sharing the hotel with Team England. Even Martin Johnson's baby is practically three feet long. The men in white glow with confidence. Surrounded by their families – Mike Catt's baby daughter is particularly cute – there is an air of grown-up calm and utter professionalism. And fair play, they all seem nice chaps. Jonny Wilkinson is polite and serious, analysing the detail of his pre-kick ritual with the intensity of a studious sixth-former describing his favourite maths equation. Clive Woodward still manages to get right up the collective Welsh nostril, however. His view is that Wales have done England a favour by suddenly turning on the style. 'It's given us an added fear factor in the camp which is always a good thing,' he smiles. 'We're a team that performs better under pressure.'

Friday November 7

Head to the Welsh team hotel to hear Steve Hansen's selection. Spot a gaggle of players en route, including Gareth Cooper and Dafydd Jones, who have both dyed tufts of their hair scarlet. Among the fans, pub debate has centred on Hansen's back-row dilemma all week, while the inclusion of Shane Williams has been deemed a must. Travelling supporter Joe Davies of Pontypridd had more advice for the Welsh coach. 'We've just got to forget the usual England–Wales thing and treat this as any other world cup quarter final,' he muses. There is more thoughtful punditry from Joe before he pauses over his pint of Victoria Bitter. 'And then we've just got to stuff it up their arses'. At the press conference, there is a more considered approach but Hansen hasn't gone for the conservative selection predicted by the hacks. Feel a little shiver as he dismisses the usual psychological baggage of an England-Wales clash with a closing comment: 'We're interested in creating our own history.' I tell team manager Alan Phillips he'd better deliver the goods as I've spent a fortune staying an extra week. David Moffett grins: 'If we do you'll have to stay another week after that.'

∙∙

Saturday November 8

Meet up with Cath Jenkins, 38, a referee from Porth and ex-pat Sylvia, 65, who originally hails from Ynyshir. In the Irish pub Gilhooleys, a Scottish and an Aussie piper perform an impromptu duet, segueing from 'Flower of Scotland' into 'Waltzing Matilda'. They repeat the performance every time a gang of English lads in the corner start bellowing 'Swing Low'. After a spending spree in A-Mart Sports, where all the Rugby World Cup goodies are beginning to be slashed in price, we catch a train to the Suncorp Stadium. We haven't got tickets for Australia v Scotland but are told the best place to watch this and the preceding New Zealand v South Africa match is Caxton Street. This turns out to be a wild-west style strip of bars housed in Colonial buildings. In the crush of gold and navy shirts there is no chance of seeing the big screen but as the Haka dies away, Sylvia has a cunning plan and bundles us into a taxi. We draw up at the entrance of the Brisbane Broncos Rugby League club. It is an impressive complex of bars, function rooms, restaurants and a mini-casino. There are two giant screens in the half-empty sports bar, one showing the match, the other a trotting race. Clutching betting slips, most of the punters are more interested in the latter. Return to Gilhooleys for the Australia v Scotland match. With the scores level at half-time the Wallabies could have been in serious trouble if the much-maligned Scots had some decent backs. By 2am the Welsh fans' optimism is flowing as freely as the VB. 'This is the first time I've been out of Splott,' beams Darren Patterson, 28, who has saved hard for the tour. 'We're going to win. All the signs are there. We beat England 16–3 in the quarter-finals in 1987 in Brisbane. And here we are again. It's our destiny.'

Sunday November 9

Woken by parents' phone call. They've been to Saturday evening mass so church won't clash with the match. The entire parish of St Gabriel & Raphael, Tonypandy, have the same idea. 'I can see where you'll all be on Sunday morning,' laughs the priest, surveying the packed pews. I just hope he offered up a few extra Hail Marys.

Leave the hotel to head for the match, fighting my way through a foyer teeming with white shirts. The England bus is parked outside as rows of fans wait to see off their team. Just a pair of red jerseys break up the sea of white – Clive and Margaret Rowlands. Grateful for some Cymric company I stop for a chat. They're the only tourists in their group who've put a winning scoreline for Wales into the sweep. At the Suncorp Stadium Welsh fans are swamped by the Barmy Army. The England supporters have been entirely good-natured. Sadly, on this occasion I'm sitting in front of three obnoxious prats, who boo the arrival of the Welsh team, find it hilarious that more than one Jones is in the line-up and ask if the mascot is our captain. When Robert Sidoli's face fills the big screen during the anthem with a single tear running down his cheek, they jeer: 'Look at that f*****g nonsense!' Five minutes later as Sid snatches an England throw in, I turn and tell them: 'See – that's what crying in the anthem does'. Their aggressive banter continues until the second Welsh try when they fall strangely silent. This could also be because their view of the match is blocked by me having a celebratory piggy-back from Terry while screaming 'Wa-hales!'

Half-time comes and with it a dream that is almost too overwhelming to contemplate. We could win this match. But then the backlash begins. Running as if he has a scorpion down his shorts, Jason Robinson creates a stunning try. 'Are Wales turning up in the second half?' quip the Chuckle Brothers. I round on them: 'Look boys, you've had 65 per cent possession, you should have put 30 points on us by now but you haven't. And you're the world cup favourites, remember?' They apologise meekly. Wales rally once more. It's three tries to one but Wilkinson's boot kills the dream. I have tears in my eyes as the Welsh boys circuit the pitch, applauding the fans. We couldn't have asked them for more. The mobile bleeps with a text message winging its way from the bar of Glynneath RFC. It's from Max. Just a single word that sums up Wales in the 2003 Rugby World Cup: 'HEROIC'.

Gareth Llewellyn salutes the fans at Brisbane
after Wales's heroic world cup campaign

WALES
PLAY IN RED

Chapter 4

Gentlemen and Players

These are a few of my favourite things.
Maria Von Trapp

• •

*T*his chapter is devoted to some of my favourite players in Welsh rugby and the characters who have lifted the game. The first sighting of a player who goes on to be something special is always interesting with hindsight. A fresh-faced Shane Williams certainly grabbed his chance to impress in 2000 as Wales faced Italy in the Six Nations for the first time.

Young Gun Shane stars in Spaghetti Western

He rode into our valley in the winter of 2000, a small man dressed in red.

'Call me Shane,' he said. He never told us more.

There was much excitement in the valley that winter, a slow, climbing tension that seemed to focus on Shane.

'There's something about him,' Mother said, 'something… dangerous…'

'He's dangerous all right,' Father said, 'but not to us… just to them pesky Italians.'

(With apologies to Jack Warner Schaefer)

THE diminutive Alan Ladd played the gunslinger called Shane, the enigmatic hero of Schaefer's classic western. And we had a lad called Shane of similar dimensions playing the role of young gun to perfection on Saturday. Shane Williams's cheekily adventurous performance proved sport can still provide storybook moments of magic. His dream debut (we'll forget about the five minutes against France) gave us all a nice, warm feeling because it satisfied many of the romantic Welsh rugby principles we hold dear.

For a start, there's the size-doesn't-matter principle. We like our wings to be fleet-footed philosophers not stampeding 17-stone juggernauts. Give us the slinky-hipped Gerald Davies magic over the Jonah Lomu battering ram any day. Small but perfectly formed Shane certainly outperformed his chunky rival Stoica.

Then there's the rugby *Roy of the Rovers* touch. Comic strip sporting heroes are always fast-tracked into the limelight after grabbing their single chance to impress and never have anything less than a Keith Jarret-esque debut to remember. Every time Shane broke into a sprint, let alone got near the ball, the faithful worked themselves into a frenzy of anticipation. Graham Henry had warned us not to burden the debutant with unreasonable expectation but he seemed to thrive on it. His kick ahead led to the line-out that gave Scott Quinnell his try; his own try was an easy stroll-over but he relished every second with the now customary young gun salute and then there was the move that for a moment, at least, looked as if it would earn the Neath flier a lifetime of action replays.

Shane was a 100-yard dash away from the stuff of misty-eyed recollection 20 years from now. As it is, the range of options he could have plumped for will probably be discussed for the next month. When it didn't come off, the look of amused disappointment on his face was straight out of the Jonathan Davies School of Enterprise and Cheeky Chappiness – I fluffed it, but at least I had a go.

So how was it for him? 'I didn't have many nerves – all the boys were talking me through the game,' he explained in the post-match interview. Not just talking – never was a new cap the focus of so much team-spirited hair-ruffling, back-slapping and general cwtching. The old hands looked positively paternalistic. He may be about to celebrate his 23rd birthday but with that cherubic face an alternative career awaits as a boy-band pin-up. 'I come from the same place as Shane Williams' was overheard as a chat-up line on Saturday night, which made me chortle almost as much as the banner: 'Aberdare Girls Live Fast – Dai Young'.

If it was a day to remember for Shane, the Italians won't forget their first Six Nations encounter with Wales in a hurry. Coach Brad Johnstone used his deadpan wit to cope with the post-match press conference, but then, anyone who has to dress up like a muscular Frank Spencer to watch the game must have a good sense of humour. It would have been nice if the pre-match entertainment reflected what was, after all, a bit of history in the making. How about a little Neopolitan opera next time? 'Just One Cornetto' would have made all the difference. Who knows what the Italian fans made of it all, as they were the least visible visitors the stadium has seen. Eighty per cent of the 6,000 tickets sent to Italy were returned yet most Azzurri fans probably got to Westgate Street via Ton Pentre rather than Treviso. Wales's great Bracchi tradition has spawned a generation with split loyalties. Take it from someone who last watched Wales v Italy at Stradey sitting next to *Western Mail* colleague Mario Basini. One minute it was 'Kick it Neil!' the next 'Avanti Massimo!'

No allegiance difficulties in a fortnight's time of course, just the small matter of overcoming the championship favourites. When Alan Ladd whizzed off into the sunset, little Joey was left hollering: 'Come back Shane!' Let's hope the England backs will be shouting the same.

February 21, 2000

· ·

Iestyn Time to Save Welsh Rugby

*I*n August 2001 the WRU brought rugby league golden boy Iestyn Harris to Wales – the deal cost a cool £1.5m. They saw it as payback time for 100 years of league raids on union:

'Today we make history,' said Glanmor Griffiths. 'This is a red letter day for our game, the boot is on the other foot now'. When Harris scored 31 points on his dazzling full debut for Cardiff, it seemed he might just be worth the investment. But we were already heaping on the pressure...

AS someone who occasionally dabbles in sports writing, it's always a thrill to be asked for an informed analysis of the Welsh rugby scene. 'So,' asked the *Western Mail* security guard, 'What do you think of Iestyn's legs then?'

Funny. I always get the thighs question. You never hear that sort of thing on *Scrum V*. 'So Jonathan, were you particularly impressed with the pertness of Gavin Henson's buns this afternoon?' 'No Ed, but I did notice Arwel Thomas is a tad blonder this season. Suits him, mind.'

That's not to say I haven't been casting a glance at Iestyn Harris's legs. And Iestyn's silver boots. And Iestyn's hands. And Iestyn's jinking hips. And Iestyn's friendly grin. But I'm not the only one on Iestyn Watch. Almost 10,000 pairs of eyes were trained on the former rugby league golden boy at the Arms Park this weekend as he made his full union debut. He's gone straight for the No 10 glamour jersey and by Christmas he could be the Beckham of Wales, minus the awful jewellery and the Twiglet wife, but with the equivalent talent and adored status.

It's both endearing and slightly disturbing how quickly icons are created in Wales. Before Iestyn's starring role on Saturday, we were given a cameo performance at Stradey. After playing his first 40 minutes of union, he was hailed as the new Barry John. Yikes, at least let the boy play a full match! He's also gone straight into the Biblical Metaphor League, the highest compliment from the Welsh rugby faithful. Graham Henry was The Great Redeemer, Iestyn is alternately The Prodigal Son – because it's rugby league pay-back time – or The Saviour, because, let's face it, we're desperate.

So can Iestyn really give us a glimpse of the Promised Land?

The weight of expectation hung over the Arms Park like a giant barrage balloon. Two small fans in blue and black walking down Westgate Street to the Cardiff v Glasgow game were in no doubt they were about to witness some Harry Potter-style wizardry. Thumping each other on the arms in the way that seven-year-old boys like to punctuate their conversation, it was Harris this, Harris that.

They didn't have to wait long. Iestyn's silver boot landed a penalty within five minutes. It's fair to say that Cardiff spectators are usually a rather reserved lot, neither known for their effervescence in moments of excitement nor generosity towards players who slip up. Saturday was different. Iestyn's first try got a standing ovation. The rare errors he made were greeted with the sort of warm indulgence new parents show towards the baby who has just stuck a piece of toast in the video. By the time he'd clocked up 31 solo points, including a hat-trick of dancing tries and created a try for Anthony Sullivan with a cross kick of sublime accuracy, the ground was emoting more than Oprah Winfrey on speed.

Union convert Iestyn Harris – payback for 100 years of League raids?

Iestyn Harris's full rugby union debut was a definite 'I Was There' sporting moment. The hype machine will now hit top gear and generate the optimistic hysteria that is a Welsh speciality.

But let him have his celebrity status. It's time we had a nice new Welsh icon to cheer us up. Taff Pop's on the wane, Catherine Zeta's frocks get more attention than her thespian attributes, Anthony Hopkins is American and Helen from *Big Brother* is only famous because she likes blinking, she does. Iestyn, meanwhile, has the one quality that should always send you to the top of the A-list – talent. He also seems sensible enough to cope with the unreasonable demands that will undoubtedly be heaped on him in the months to come. If only we could be sensible too. When spell-checking this column, the computer offered an interesting alternative for the 'unknown word' Iestyn – it suggested 'destiny'. After 120 minutes of rugby union, we've already placed the fate of the Welsh game on his shoulders. It's a heavy burden.

October 29, 2001

Top Cat – the Man who made Rugby equal Welshness

Clive Rowlands is the only man to have captained, coached and managed the Welsh rugby team and acted as WRU President. He's also one of the great characters of the game whose passion for Wales, rugby and the delights of Upper Cwmtwrch is infectious

IF Welsh identity were a drink most of us now plump for Cymru Lite. It's a sophisticated tipple encompassing the spirit of modern Welsh life – slickly marketed and devoid of potentially embarrassing cliches. Cardiff Bay not Tiger Bay; Ioan rather than Burton and the Welsh Mam covers her bump in stretch Gucci and hangs off the arm of Michael Douglas.

75

Preachers are of the Manic Street variety rather than Bethesda brimstone and fire. History is filleted for promotional purposes with a selectivity that went down well in Stalinist Russia. So while Owain Glyndŵr is cool, miners are so last century, *cariad*. We could do more to exploit the tourism potential of our industrial heritage but it's better to keep them under wraps. Wouldn't want all those dirty faces, hard hats and lamps turning up on the National Lottery Show again would we? Past rugby glory just burdens the poor players of the present. And as for Male Voice Choirs, unless you can add some blissed-out beats to 'Myfanwy' or give those blazers a touch of retro post-modern styling then it's so long to sol-fa.

Yet sometimes it's refreshing to take a deep draught of Full Strength Welshness and not be uncomfortable with the unashamed richness, warmth and sentiment of it. FSW was on tap at the celebration of Clive Rowlands's life and career on Friday night. The legends of British rugby turned up at Cardiff's Coal Exchange to pay homage to Top Cat on the 40th anniversary of his first Welsh cap. Scotland's Ian McGeechan and England's Roger Uttley voiced their tributes alongside the Welsh stars of the game. From tales of how Clive motivated his team to 'believe in the dream' to how his rolling gait on the field could make him look 'like John Wayne with piles' – complete with actions from Gareth Edwards – the anecdotes ranged from moving to hilarious.

Prince Charles sent his appreciation in letter form: 'This comes with my boundless admiration and warmest good wishes to Clive on this very special anniversary,' he wrote. 'I know that life more recently has been less easy for Clive as he has fought against cancer, but he has done this with the courage for which he is renowned.' HRH closed his tribute by describing Clive's immense talents as an 'ambassador for Wales'.

Almost every speaker reiterated the theme of the night. Top Cat equalled rugby and he made rugby equal Welshness. To him the root of this equation lay in the community. When he won his first cap all of Upper Cwmtwrch were there in spirit. 'Everybody in my village

A cwtch from Clive 'Top Cat' Rowlands and his wife Margaret on the 2001 Lions Tour   *(Carolyn Hitt)*

wanted to go on there as well. I was the one representing them.' Clive has described the wondrous realms of UC to me many times. When 200 Welsh fans were stranded in Rome airport for five hours this year, he entertained them in the aisles with his full repertoire of UC gags. The village had taken on an almost mythical status in my mind – thanks in part to a very long joke he tells involving UC and Princess Anne – but that didn't stop me missing the turning when I went there to interview him. Running very late and totally lost in the nether regions of Ystradgynlais, I called his wife Margaret: 'Don't worry. He's waiting for you down by the sign.'

And there was Clive, a one-man welcoming committee sitting patiently in his car on the border between Upper and Lower Cwmtwrch. If I'd been crossing the Bering Strait, the moment could not have had more geographical significance.

I interviewed Clive about his legendary team-talks for a radio series on sports psychology. He said his motivational oratory – in which he invoked everyone from 'Aunty Mabel to Owain Glyndŵr' in willing his players to win – was influenced by the chapel minister of his childhood. On Friday night the anecdotes about these rousing rugby sermons came thick and fast. 'He'd say "Who's worn that jersey before you?"' recalled Gerald Davies, '"There's a long lineage before you and that's the jersey you're wearing today." It made you feel ten feet tall. The essence of Welsh rugby is instilled in him.' Gareth Edwards said Clive's team-talks were 'all about the ticker.' And in summing up he underlined why Cymru Lite still has a lot to learn from Full Strength Welshness. 'Clive really put Welsh rugby on a pedestal which the present players should be proud of because if you don't know where you've been, how the hell do you know where you're going?'

September 15, 2003

The True Grit of the Ginger Monster

There's something about red-haired sons of Ponty – Neil Jenkins and Martyn Williams remain two of my biggest rugby heroes. When Jenks hung up his boots, I wanted to pay tribute to one of the nice guys of sport as well as one of the most talented.

SINCE Neil Jenkins announced his retirement from the game his career highlights have been listed many times, from his kicking heroics on the 1997 Lions Tour to the nerveless conversion that sealed that wondrous Wembley win. But I'll always connect the Ginger Monster with a damp Saturday morning in Aberdare. It was a match during the 1999 Rugby World Cup between two under-11 sides with all the ingredients of classic schoolboy rugby.

There was the youngster belting towards the line pursued by his entire back division screaming for a pass. He may have been the most well-supported player since Anna Kournikova signed a deal with Berlei Sportsbras, but there was no way he was going to let his teammates deprive him of solo glory.

There was the prop who had already acquired all the accoutrements of front-row kudos – a scowl, a scrum-cap and a fearsome nickname. 'We call him The Terminator,' said my nephew in reverent tones. And there were the maniacal adults puffing up and down the touchline, bellowing tactical advice and the odd Anglo Saxon expression in the direction of the referee – and those were just the mothers.

But then came a moment of grown-up rugby. The touchline parents fell silent as a munchkin-sized outside half prepared to take a penalty. The ritual began. Four steps back, two steps left and a glance up at the posts. Pause. A look at the ball and then two shuddering movements of the hands like a conductor teasing a poignant chord from his orchestra. Pause. Kick.

As the ball sailed through the air for a split second this 10-year-old boy believed he was Neil Jenkins . . . until he missed by the proverbial mile.

Watching a youngster attempting to emulate his hero was a heartening sight. This kid knew the future was orange. A generation of junior Ginger Monsters have grown up knowing that if they want to be the best goal kickers in the world they have to practise as much as Jenks did. He's shown them they need other qualities too. There's the mental toughness required to endure the verbal knocks. As Neil himself once said, 'Nowhere else gives the outside half as much stick as here.' There were times when he got enough stick to build a bonfire, but each time he was roasted, the Ponty phoenix dragged himself from the ashes and flew once more.

The same inner strength could be seen on the pitch when he cocooned himself from baying crowds with his pre-kick ceremony. And it wasn't as if stress-control came naturally – his pre-match queasiness is the stuff of legend. But above all, Jenks showed them how they should conduct themselves off the pitch. As the player who always had time for the last autograph hunter, however golden his boots became he never got too big for them.

There can be no better role model for the foot soldiers coming through the ranks than the man who put the valour into Valley Commando.

May 31, 2004

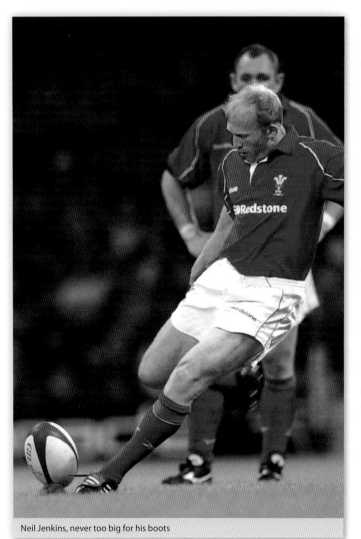

Neil Jenkins, never too big for his boots

78

The Toughest Centre with the Softest Heart

*T*he rugby world wept in October 2007 when we lost Ray Gravell. Well-loved doesn't even begin to describe the affection in which he was held.

I STILL can't believe Grav has gone. All that energy and humour, passion and patriotism. His tenderness and courage. His sheer zest for life. How can all that just cease so cruelly? The toughest centre with the softest heart, a doting dad and affectionate friend, he was unique.

On the morning Wales woke up to the tragic news of Grav's sudden death, I watched the message boards on Radio Wales fill with tributes. These weren't the usual stock phrases of condolence. Almost every listener wanted to explain how he had touched his or her life. They all had an anecdote they wanted to share – for even a brief meeting with Grav would leave the most lasting impression.

When he was recovering from surgery, he and his wife Mari were overwhelmed with the scale of the response, as cards and letters from across the world found their way to Heol Ray Gravell, Mynedd-y-Garreg. Such an outpouring of warmth was no surprise to the rest of us. We were just trying to return the favour. Grav was a tonic in human form. He always made you feel better – whether it was with a generous compliment, an enthusiastic chat or just a

huge bear hug. It now seems especially poignant that Wales got the chance to tell Grav just how much he was loved. Completely without ego, he never seemed to realise just how special he was. He was always too busy telling other people why they should feel good about themselves.

Like so many, I frequently experienced the joy of a Grav pep talk. When I was first asked to write about rugby, even though I loved the game I still worried that I wasn't qualified to hold an opinion. But each time I bumped into Grav our motivational routine was the same. I would get a hug, he'd tell me how much he had enjoyed that week's piece and if someone happened to be passing at the same time he would grab them and tell them why they should read it too. It was such a lovely confidence boost.

Ray Gravell – legend, hero and friend   (Carolyn Hitt)

I watched him show that same generosity of spirit as he gave a speech before Wales's world cup game against Australia. The room was filled with corporate movers and shakers but there was also a family who had won competition tickets to the match. And Grav ensured their youngest member – a 13-year-old Scarlets fan – was treated like the star guest. Throughout his talk he kept throwing lines in the boy's direction, addressing him by name as the youngster beamed with pride.

He was such a magical communicator. Who can forget those tactile touchline interviews, those last minute pats on players' backs as they ran out of the tunnel and those hilarious turns of phrase as Gavin Henson was told he was 'cool for cats' or Scottish coach Matt Williams was greeted with 'Here he is – Robert Redford!' His irrepressible broadcasting style was an antidote to the cynical side of professional sport.

All of Wales feels his loss but, of course, our grief cannot compare with that of Mari and his daughters Manon and Gwenan. I'll never forget talking to Grav about his girls while on the Lions tour of Australia. His eyes filled with tears as he explained how much he was missing them. He was the ultimate family man.

Grav embodied all the ideals we'd like Welsh rugby to represent – the romanticism, the passion, the camaraderie, the dignity, the bond between player and fan, the immense pride in the jersey. Ray Gravell is irreplaceable but the greatest tribute Wales could pay him would be to ensure the values he cherished live on in our national game.

November 2, 2007

Gavin Henson – Hero or Villain?

I feel like I've been defending Gavin Henson since he bought his first tub of hair gel. Perhaps it's because I first interviewed him as the shy 19-year-old who had just been crowned IRB Junior World Player of the Year. I've spent the last 11 years hoping he would fulfil that potential to the full. This stab at explaining the enigma of Gav was written as he attempted to revive his playing career after an extended reality television sabbatical. He admitted with a grin that after reading it he wasn't sure himself which he was...

GAVIN Henson – hero or villain? While the truth about Welsh rugby's greatest enigma lies somewhere between these extremes, opinion of him is more polarised than ever.

For every romantic dreaming of the Prodigal Son gliding back into the squad to inspire Wales to world cup glory there is a grumpy old man sneering he is a one-kick wonder.

For every marketing guru impressed with how Henson has built his brand there is a cynic rolling his eyes at the Faustian pact he signed with the celebrity devil.

For every female who warmed to his metrosexual man-grooming there is a male distraught that any normal Welsh bloke would be interested in depilatory methods.

Fascinating. Infuriating. Exhilarating. Exasperating. Overrated. Underrated. Misunderstood. Maddening. Or as one rugby writer once quipped: 'He's trouble, but not more trouble than he's worth.' It all depends on your personal response to the Cult of Gavin. What is certain is that Henson remains a paradox. From the moment he first laced his up his golden boots he has tied us in knots with his mixed messages.

Arrogance and introversion are rarely qualities shared by one personality, yet both have played their part in the Henson psyche. As the teenager crowned the World Young Player of the Year he was so shy his Swansea coach made him work at St Helen's reception to mingle with the public and draw him out of himself. Yet on the pitch – hair skewered into spikes and skin burnished with a tangerine glow in the depths of a West Glamorgan winter – his appearance screamed: 'Look at me'.

Throughout his career the contradictions have continued. He loves media attention yet feels persecuted by the press. Gnarled old forwards were bemused by an image that was almost effete yet his legend grew from acts of supreme on-field machismo.

He is known for his body beautiful yet that meticulously honed form has endured endless ugly injuries. He has been ignored by coaches and courted by coaches. Deified by fans and demonised by fans. And in his nature, his soft side has been occasionally subsumed by his dark side.

Across pages of *OK!* magazine he presented himself as the doting dad, maturity enhanced by the responsibilities of fatherhood. But just as we were cooing at Henson the New Man ensconced in domestic bliss, Henson the beer monster would pop up on a pool table in a Cardiff pub, his rowdiness forcing Mike Phillips to seize a karaoke microphone and apologise for his behaviour.

Alleged incidents on the First Great Western, and getting so grand slammed after Wales's championship triumph in 2005 he ended up needing a lift home from the police, have added to the wild boy reputation. But the irony remains that Henson is not a big drinker and looks after his body with the diligence of the obsessive athlete.

Yet that dedication to the physical brings us to another inconsistency. Rugby is in the very DNA of this son of a Maesteg prop. But sometimes you wonder whether the Henson who picked up his first rugby ball at five was smothering himself in greasepaint rather than Deep Heat, such has been the lure of limelight over floodlight.

There have been so many times when Henson the celeb has smothered Henson the player in much the same way as the latter scooped up and dumped Mathew Tait into the

Millennium turf. So just when we thought he was ready to return to the oval ball after a self-imposed sabbatical of 19 months the glitter ball twirled into view and whisked him on to the dance floor – his third sortie into reality television that year.

But from the start Henson had self-confessed designs on being the Beckham of rugby and built his brand accordingly. He is a product of his era. His rugby career would run exactly parallel with a shift in popular culture. His was a generation that would forge an entirely new relationship with celebrity as television and the media redefined the concept of fame through the growth of reality shows and personality-led press coverage.

With hindsight, when I interviewed a teenage Henson on his aspirations, there were already signs that this changing environment was an influence. The likeable youngster,

Gavin Henson (left) and Gareth Thomas, heroes of victory over England at Cardiff in 2005

who described his interest in designer fashion and facial products, insisted on wearing a hat because he hadn't realised there would be a photographer and he hadn't 'done his hair.'

Asked to name his rugby hero, he cited David Campese. This was an intriguing choice of idol. Campo wasn't just a maverick on the field, he was known for a controversial turn of phrase and was arguably the game's first player to perceive himself as a commodity, famously boasting 'I'm still an amateur, of course, but I became rugby's first millionaire five years ago .'

Henson also knew his own market value, exploiting his Grand Slam Year in a premature ghosted autobiography, collecting lucrative endorsements and sponsorships and falling for a girlfriend with equal profile.

Around him, young people were being sold the dream of instant celebrity and achievement without any real graft. The icons of a previous era were seen to have worked their way to the top – fame came as a by-product of their talent. But the *Big Brother/Heat*-magazine-reading generation knew it took much less effort to be famous for just being famous.

The irony of Henson, of course, is that unlike his generation of wannabe C-listers he does have genuine talent. Yet while his public image is undoubtedly rooted in sporting accomplishment, somewhere along the line the balance between rugby and celebrity tipped.

The choice of Campese as a role model also throws light on another aspect of Henson's personality that has mired him in controversy – his honesty. 'He's quality. He's arrogant but in a good way,' said the teenage Henson of Campo. 'He's great to watch, you see other people giving the same old interview. You know what they're going to say and most of it's rubbish, but with him it's different, you don't know what he's going to say and it's always exciting.'

Much the same could be said of Henson himself. He's always given great soundbite. Who can forget his description of Alistair Campbell's ill-advised attempt at a post-match team-talk on the disastrous 2005 Lions Tour. 'It was unbelievable crap,' declared the player treated pretty shoddily by both the spin doctor and coach Clive Woodward. 'As a player you can take this sort of stuff from ex-internationals but where was Campbell coming from… it was rubbish and it backfired badly.'

But not as badly as the book itself which caused uproar among the Welsh teammates Henson had discussed in its pages with similar candour. Such apparent unconcern for the feelings of others has been the main reason Henson has been accused of egotism over the years yet there is a sense that it is more about innocence than arrogance. His need to speak the truth seems to blind him to the consequences.

He was genuinely taken aback by the furore over his book. 'Seriously, I believe that I'm an honest person,' he said at the time. 'There's nothing really complicated about me so I just tried to tell it as I saw it.'

• •

He also didn't see what all the fuss was about when he agreed to model the new Welsh kit last autumn. Accepting the rather disingenuous WRU marketing line that he was helping promote grassroots rugby, he was bemused by the fact some current players might feel miffed he was the Chosen One given he's been so far from the squad in recent times you'd need an Admiral's telescope to locate him.

Henson is better in person than print or 100ft poster form. While the Welsh rugby community lost patience with his celebrity sabbatical, it may have done him some good, changing perceptions of his personality. A certain bashful charm emerged on the *Strictly* dance floor, while on *71 Degrees North* the vanity he is often charged with was revealed to be largely tongue-in-cheek and part of his appeal.

He's a lot brighter than people give him credit for too. Henson's deadpan wit warmed many an icy Norwegian night. But the strength of his competitive spirit left the largest imprint on the celebrity snow. And if that is still what drives him then his ambitions to make a return to elite rugby should be supported rather than derided.

For beneath the tan, the tantrums and the trappings of fame lies a diehard rugby player of instinct and talent. His detractors reduce his achievements to one kick and the up-ending of Mathew Tait. But from the moment he sparkled on to the scene as a teen on a Santiago rugby pitch – all Puckish hair and impassive face – it was obvious here was a player of singular ability.

In the autumn of 2004, as Wales came agonisingly close to beating the All Blacks and South Africa, he was sublime, a player of soft hands, strong tackles and gliding breaks. His subtle creative skills and huge defensive abilities were also integral to the Welsh Grand Slams of 2005 and 2008.

He should be a member of the 50-cap brigade yet he's never even been to a world cup. But is celebrity really to blame for Henson veering between either end of the Jekyll and Hyde scale of public opinion?

The real reason so much attention has been focused on what he gets up to off the pitch is because he's never had the chance to enjoy an uninterrupted career on it. Sadly having endured a succession of hernia, groin, Achilles tendon, ankle and calf injuries, his script is more Holby City than Hollywood.

Henson has suffered emotionally from the physical setbacks he has been dealt. Without these soul-sapping injuries who knows how different his story might have been. If his body had remained intact we certainly wouldn't have spent so much time trying to work out what was going on in his head.

So, villain? No. I'll hold out for the hero Gavin Henson once was… and still could be.

March 2011

Holding out for the hero:
Gavin Henson holds up another high-profile
international centre, Brian O'Driscoll of Ireland

. . . .

Nugget of Pure Gold

I'M often asked who my favourite player is. Women are expected to pick the glamour back either on purely aesthetic grounds or because if you're blonde they assume you'll find it easier to spot the wing flying over the try line rather than unravel the macho mysteries of what goes on in the engine room.

But while I have an undeniable soft spot for the sparkle of Shane, it's the other Williams who has always captured my rugby heart – flame-haired flanker Martyn. The man they call Nugget – so often the only flash of pure gold when Wales were getting panned – is the embodiment of Valleys grit.

His 1999 switch from Ponty to Cardiff further developed him as a player but as a person he didn't buy into the flasher side of professional rugby. Indeed he never forgot his Sardis Road heritage. If there is one anecdote that illustrates this it is the story my nephew tells of the time he and his teammates at Ponty Youth won the league. The young players were beside themselves that Nugget himself was the guest of honour at their end-of-season presentation night.

But that excitement was nothing compared to the positive awe they felt when one of the best flankers on the planet finished off the formalities by saying: 'C'mon boys, let's go and have a drink.' Being taken into town for some celebratory bevvies by their hero is a memory they will cherish forever.

He gave us all memories to savour. On the eve of the Oscars in 2005, he deserved his own Academy Award for rewriting the script in Stade de France. Who can forget the way he single-handedly put Wales back in the Grand Slam frame with those two lightning-swift tries. Enticed out of international retirement by Warren Gatland, the former Welsh captain played a similarly integral role in the 2008 Grand Slam campaign.

Physically, he didn't fit the template of the modern game's muscular behemoths. Martyn is perhaps the only rugby player who looks like an ordinary bloke on civvy street – no bulging biceps to strain the Eden Park leisurewear.

He was still an extraordinary presence on the field, however, with his deft link play, breakdown scavenging and an ability to read the game that suggested he was scanning four analysis laptops simultaneously up in the coaches' box rather than considering options in the heat of the battle.

But what has made his sporting success all the more remarkable is the subtext of family sadness that has accompanied his rugby journey.

Some of the highest points in Martyn's career have run parallel with the darkest periods in his personal life. In a chapter of his biography entitled 'Losing the Ones you Love', Martyn outlines the double tragedy of the deaths of his mother and younger brother Craig to cancer. Craig died within three months of diagnosis in 2000, aged just 18.

The black-eyed Nugget, pursued by teammate Adam Jones

Although devastated, Martyn vowed to channel his grief in a positive way. 'I'll admit there were days after Craig passed away when I was thinking, "What's the point, it's only a game?" But I knew he wouldn't have wanted me to think like that and I drew strength from him. I also wanted to achieve something to give my parents something to take their minds off their loss, because I could see how much they were hurting. So I threw everything into it and, six months later, I found myself on the British Lions tour of Australia… from the moment I was selected I decided to dedicate that trip to Craig, because he had been the one to give me the strength to carry on.'

Five years later his mother was diagnosed with incurable cancer. 'She was only 47 and, coming after what had happened to Craig, it just seemed so unfair and so cruel,' wrote Martyn. So at a time when he was hitting the heights with Wales's Grand Slam-winning side – notching up the performances that earned him the Player of the Tournament prize – he was enduring desperate lows on the home front.

'When I look back at 2005, it seems so strange. It brought me everything I wanted in my rugby career yet, off the field, I also went through the worst time of my life,' he wrote. 'It's hard for me to put into words just how much my mother did for me and just how big a part she played in my life.'

Martyn believes the sense of perspective gained from his bereavements has helped him as a player. 'It makes you realise that family is everything, and everything you do is ultimately for them.'

The strength of character the Wales and Blues icon has shown in these devastating circumstances make him a truly inspirational sportsman. As he says himself 'Yes, rugby matters, but life matters more.'

July 2012

Ginger, brown and black and blue: Martyn Williams in Cardiff colours

. . . .

Shane – a 5ft 7ins Metaphor for Wales itself

One of the first rugby columns I ever wrote was on the Graham Henry trial match that saw Shane Williams fast-tracked into his 2000 Six Nations squad. Although it was obvious the Neath flier was an electric talent who could have predicted his retirement would feel like such a massive national milestone. But then, Shane is Wales...

EVEN in his very first team picture for Amman United Juniors a cherubic Shane Williams – barely reaching the shoulder of the lad next to him – looked like the mascot alongside his fellow schoolboys.

On his full debut for Wales the image was much the same. Like a first former whose mother has bought his uniform with built-in growing room, Shane wore a jersey large enough to accommodate himself and a Quinnell.

But the excess of red material didn't impede his aerodynamics. He announced himself to international rugby with a stroll-over try and a cheeky young gun salute. As his teammates smothered the new cap with paternal hugs, a smile spread across the face of the Welsh rugby public. They knew a classic Welsh jinker when they saw one and instantly took him to their bosom.

We loved him because he was a 5ft 7ins metaphor for Wales itself. While England celebrated the beetle-browed doggedness of a Johnson and New Zealand cherished the powerful back-row brawn of a McCaw, Little Shane was the player who made our hearts beat faster.

For when he shimmied around men twice his size and turned all the accepted wisdom of the modern professional game on its head, he took us to the core of why rugby matters to Wales. It gives a small nation the chance to be on top of the world. Punching way above his weight on the global stage, Shane's international career embodied the message that if you've got enough talent size doesn't matter.

In the wake of Shane's first season Welsh Milk turned him into their poster boy – remember those bus-stop white moustaches? – but his dream of more caps turned sour when Graham Henry refused to pick him. Shane didn't get a game in 2002, an injustice that may have prevented him from hanging up his Welsh boots with the try-scoring world record to add to his many other accolades.

Henry's successor had similar misgivings about Shane's diminutive stature even though the land of three million selectors begged to differ. 'Tell him to make sure Shane's on the plane,' insisted my mother as I went to interview Steve Hansen before the 2003 World Cup.

Hansen did take him – but only as third-choice scrum half. Yet what a crucial decision it turned out to be as Shane electrified Wales's world cup campaign, dazzling in those games against the All Blacks and England. As the back pages of the Australian press declared, 'Dragons Scare the Not-So-Mighty All Blacks', praise was heaped on Shane – as well as wonderment at the dimensions of Wales's pocket dynamo. He was referred to as 'The 77kg Winger' throughout the tournament.

Shane was back. And his return to the international scene was testament to an inner steel that made him refuse to be written off. Olympic gold medallist Lynn Davies, someone who knows a thing or too about the psychology of the elite sportsman, believes Shane's mindset makes him as special as his physical gifts.

'His mental attitude has always been very positive, he has great mental toughness,' said Lynn. 'He was told he was too small to play rugby and adopted an "I'll show them" approach. He applied total, almost Olympic, commitment to strength training which allowed him to take tackles from the three big men who were committed to marking him.'

Shane Williams showing his circus skills as he scores against Scotland during the 2008 Grand Slam campaign

By the mid-noughties Shane was pure box office. On the 2004 summer tour of Argentina he showed the country that gave the world the tango how Welsh boys dance, bewildering the Puma defence with his fabulous footwork. In 2005 he squeezed into the corner against England to score the first try of a Six Nations campaign that ended with Wales's first Grand Slam for 27 years.

The wonderful cheek and flamboyance of his play was matched by a similarly adventurous approach to his appearance. He dabbled with highlights and a post-modern Mullet which made him look like a very speedy cockatiel. But then he shaved it all off, all schoolboy innocence vanishing with a mean Number One.

Perhaps it was an omen for 2008 was the season Shane was Number One, his imperious year on the field ending in the ultimate honour of being crowned IRB World Player of the Year. A second Grand Slam in four years for Wales was a collective achievement gilded with Shane's individual sparkle.

He worked his alchemy against Scotland to outrageous effect that year. After slipping tackles on an explosive run, only Nikki Walker could shackle Shane's progress by lunging for his legs. So the former gymnast showed his circus skills, sending his pins skyward and his right arm the right side of the corner flag. Emerging with an appropriate layer of greasepaint from the whitewash, Shane knew his acrobatics had done the trick.

Against Ireland for the Triple Crown, he accelerated through the Irish defence to score a similarly belief-defying – and pivotal – try in the opposite corner. The choreography of his dancing tries against Italy, meanwhile, left Shaun Edwards incredulous, mouthing his admiration up in the coaching box with three little words: 'What a player'.

Shane may have been poetry in motion throughout that campaign but it was the most prosaic of his tries that will be forever imprinted on Warren Gatland's memory: 'For me the Grand Slam try in 2008 against France where it wasn't through his running it was just his kick and chase and perseverance that did it. I'll never forget it – special memory.'

That summer his performance against South Africa left all of us with an unforgettable Shane moment. Indeed when I asked 15 Welsh greats to pay tribute to Shane for Radio Wales almost every one of them cited either his skinning of Bryan Habana in the first test or his side-stepping evasion of half the Springbok team in the second as their favourite piece of Williams magic.

'When Shane scored in Bloemfontein I was out there commentating,' recalls Ieuan Evans. 'All the Afrikaaners were simply open mouthed as he left Bryan Habana on his backside.'

According to James Dean Bradfield of the Manic Street Preachers, 'When Shane scored that try in the second test, skinning four or five South African defenders, it was the wake-up call for people beyond Europe that he was a genuine world-class talent. They now knew if you didn't try to mark him out of the game he would punish you.'

If Shane's glories in attack are well-documented, let's not forget his defensive feats which are all the more remarkable given he barely reached the collarbone of some of those he has felled.

In that surreal match against Scotland in 2010 he will be remembered as the player who scored the injury time try that sealed the most remarkable comeback in Six Nations history. Yet earlier in the game I'll never forget the way he stopped a certain Scottish try as he leapt to gather a cross-kick from Dan Parks. Competing with two taller Caledonians, Wales's shortest man on the field seemed to turn into Stretch Armstrong to pluck the ball out of the sky.

And this year in the world cup warm up victory against England he prevented Matt Banahan from scoring even though this 6ft 7ins monster has tattoos that are bigger than Shane.

All these examples of Shane's wing wizardry add up to more than a decade of dazzling entertainment. No wonder he remains the only Grogg to be crafted in flight. As rugby sculptor Richard Hughes explained, 'Balancing a Grogg on one leg is almost impossible but we had to do it for Shane.'

But then Shane himself turned rugby into an art-form. Has any other player of the modern era provided so much spectacle, style and sheer pleasure for rugby fans in Wales and beyond? His dancing odyssey through Welsh rugby has been a joy to witness and as he reaches journey's end, James Dean Bradfield beautifully sums up Shane's place in the history of our game:

'He is the quintessence of what people outside Wales imagine or want Welsh rugby to be – the romance of that off-the-cuff style of play and that buccaneering spirit. So he became the link between the present and the past. That makes him timeless and that makes him a true great.'

Shane is indeed the link between the present and the past. And as the whistle blows on his final game for Wales it is poignant to imagine a future without him. Thanks for the magic, Shane.

December 3 2011

Shane's acrobatic final try for Wales – in his final game, against Australia at the Millennium Stadium in December 2011

Chapter 5

Lions and Dragons

You can't really discuss Lions tours without the Welsh being involved.

Gareth Edwards

. . . .

The Appeal of Four Nations as One

FOR a player, joining the elite ranks of the British and Irish Lions on tour is the ultimate achievement. It's pretty good fun for the fans too. I've been lucky enough to travel on two – Australia 2001 and South Africa 2009.

They say what goes on tour stays on tour… but not when I've been around. As the Red Army marched across two continents, I sent despatches from the Lions fans' frontline.

I wasn't going to go in 2009. Credit crunch and all that. And contrary to popular belief I haven't been on one long rugby freebie for the last 15 years. Believe it or not, I actually pay for those trips. I must have invested enough in the fortunes of the Welsh team in the last decade to bail out Greece. But hey, as my mother always said, there are no pockets in a shroud. And occasionally, there's been a wonderful return.

With such a strong Welsh influence in 2009 it was hard to resist. Dot Davies and I followed Henry's Lions in Australia for the same reason. Plus the fact that Dot got five numbers on the lottery and six glasses of celebratory wine later she decided there was no better way to spend this unexpected windfall.

Woodward's Lions had less appeal because of, well, Woodward. Ignoring the sparkle of Grand Slam 2005 champions Wales, Clive based his selection on his decidedly less fizzy England world cup players who were two years past their sell-by date. And who wants to go on tour with Alistair Campbell?

But a tour led by Mr Lions himself, Ian McGeechan, not to mention Gerald and the entire Welsh coaching team, promised a return to the classic values of rugby's last great adventure. So once the squad was announced, I spent the next fortnight checking the travel website every morning with shredded nerves, hoping for a last-minute bargain. With just two places left, I finally succumbed.

Then the pre-tour build-up began. Like the players, fans also get kitted out. Sports travel companies ensure you resemble a member of a mass leisurewear cult by sending you a wondrous goodie package of pacamacs, polo shirts, flight bags and baseball caps. There's only one problem. The female form is not catered for. The garments only come in sizes suitable for a Maesteg prop forward. My all-weather jacket could quite easily have been pitched as accommodation for four at Kruger National Park.

But glamour is not a consideration on a Lions tour as you become part of one big home nations rugby tribe. It can be strange initially. Dot made me promise not to let anybody back home know she'd spent three weeks screaming for Jonny Wilkinson, Martin Johnson, and most controversially of all, Neil Back. But the blending of the nations is what makes the experience special. Supporting identities remain distinct but manage to merge beautifully too. The uniqueness of this phenomenon occurred to me around 3.30am on the last day of the Australian tour while being hoisted on the shoulders of two kilted Scotsmen as English and Irish voices sang 'Cwm Rhondda'.

That said, we Taffs do tend to dominate these expeditions. Ever since the first organised tours started emerging for the 1977 tour to New Zealand, Wales has enjoyed the Lions' share of travelling support. In 2001, incredulous Aussies kept asking us: 'Did one of you remember to turn the lights off when you left Wales?' Ceri Williams, wife of Wales team manager Alan, arrived in Sydney and told us: 'They say it's like the war in Kenfig Hill – there isn't a man left!'

When the Lions played their first Test in 2001, the Gabba stadium in Brisbane got a Cymric waistband, with dragons draped around its entire circumference. The first banner I saw 12,000 miles from home declared 'Gilfach Goch Wine Bar'. Once I'd got over the shock that Gilfach Goch actually had a wine bar, I scanned the stands for more Welsh messages. The Railway Inn, Abertillery, was also grasping the commercial nettle. Taffs Wells RFC had gone for the personal touch with a gleeful message for an absent friend: 'Thomas, we are here – you are not.'

There were other ways to keep friends and family informed of Welsh Lions fans' antics abroad – some went so far as to write their names and addresses on slips of paper and stuff them in my fleece pockets. Others wanted to keep their adventures strictly hush hush: 'Look love, the wives don't know about the stop-off in Bangkok, so keep quiet, right?'

That pre-tour detour proved particularly popular with single sex parties of males back in 2001 – it also spawned one of the great all-time Lions-tour urban myths. The story of the missing 78-year-old West Walian did the rounds. Apparently his tour mates lost him for three days in Bangkok. He allegedly turned up at the airport and introduced an 18-year-old stunner with the words, 'Meet my fiancée, boys!'

That may have been as fictional as the tale of the kangaroo who was given a Welsh rugby club blazer to wear and bounced off with the mini-bus keys in his pocket, but the escapades of Ruby and Christine, Carmarthenshire's 60-something answer to Thelma and Louise, were thoroughly factual. Roving ambassadors for wild, Welsh womanhood, this fabulous pair provided all the pre- and post-match entertainment on our tour.

Our rugby legend host Dai Watkins later admitted he didn't know what was the more scary experience – being flattened by All Black giant Colin Meads on the '66 Lions tour or giving Ruby a piggy-back up the aisle of the bus when she was somewhat worse for wear after a day's wine tasting in the Hunter Valley. The rest of us were still in shock from Christine's alternative version of 'She'll Be Coming Round The Mountain'.

Those are the kind of travelling companions that make the Lions touring experience such fantastic fun. But if you don't want your nearest and dearest discovering what you're up to, don't worry – I know what goes on tour… But if you do, just slip a note in the pocket of my Lions All Weather Supporters Jacket – there'll be plenty of room.

. . . .

Lion Kings

When Graham Henry took the helm of the 2001 Lions tour there was a nice symmetry to his leadership as the '71 Lions had fired his interest in coaching 30 years earlier. I talked to the Welsh players from the tour that changed the face of rugby.

IN the summer of 1971, a rugby-mad New Zealander in the first year of his teaching career watched the unthinkable happen. His beloved, invincible, hard-as-granite All Blacks got beaten by the British Lions for the first time. While the Lions' Test series victory may have bruised his national pride, the style of their play galvanised his personal ambitions. Thanks to the 1971 Lions, British rugby would never be the same again – and neither would a young schoolmaster called Graham Henry.

'The '71 Lions I remember very, very well,' Henry recalls. 'The great Carwyn James was the coach of their side. They set new standards of rugby, an all-round 15-man game. So I have special memories of those Lions. When I first started taking coaching seriously a few years after the '71 Tour, Carwyn and several players wrote the book *The Lions Speak* and I used that as my coaching bible. It served the foundations of my coaching career and Carwyn was a big influence on me.'

Thirty years later Henry began his own chapter in Lions history. The dominance of English players in his squad was a source of minor distress for the passionate – but unrealistic – Welsh fan. In 1971 nobody complained as the Lions left for the other side of the world with a Welsh coach, a Welsh captain and 13 Welsh members of the 30-strong squad, including six from 1970s super club London Welsh alone.

Wales provided the nucleus of the squad but the rest of the isles contributed their share of talent. 'That team had world-class players,' said Cliff Morgan, who covered the tour as a broadcaster. 'Barry John, Gareth Edwards, JPR, Gerald Davies, David Duckham, Mike Gibson, Willie John McBride and John Dawes as the perfect captain. He did for the Lions what he'd done for London Welsh and Wales.'

What Dawes had done for club and country was help pioneer a new, vibrant, attacking style of play that was sweeping through the Welsh game. The home nations had been given a sparkling sneak-preview of this rugby revolution in Wales's 1971 Grand Slam triumph. Yet for all this apparent embarrassment of riches, no-one actually expected the Lions to win.

'We left under cover of darkness with everyone saying "There go the Lions again to get a beating",' remembers Gerald Davies. 'They'd say nice things like "Well done, do your best," but they still thought we were going to get stuffed.' The British rugby-loving public had no reason to think otherwise. 'The tradition was that the Lions always lost,' explains *Sunday Times* rugby correspondent Stephen Jones. 'They had never won a Test series in New Zealand. They always had the perennial British backline brilliance and yet were traditionally poor in the forwards. It was thought vaguely un-British, even "professional", for any Lions team to do much in the way of real preparation. Vastly entertaining and yet losing. What more could any Kiwi rugby follower wish for in his visiting teams?'

So when Doug Smith, the charismatic Scottish team manager, turned soothsayer on the eve of the first match, prophesying the Lions would take the series with two wins, one loss and a draw, New Zealand deemed his crystal ball as cloudy as a wet day in Invercargill. Four months later, as Smith's prophecy was fulfilled, All Blacks glowering captain Colin Meads declared him to be 'the greatest bloody predictor of all time'.

The Lions believed the series was there for the taking from the start. 'The crucial part was winning the first test, that was the important one,' says Gerald Davies. 'We were given a drubbing by New Zealand – we shouldn't have won. They played a hard, tough, uncompromising game and they threw everything at us, but somehow we stuck in there and won. I don't think New Zealand had ever started a test series by going one down. The psychology of the teams change and it was New Zealand who had to come from behind. After that they weren't very sure how they should play it. For the first time ever they became confused, unsure who their best team were and although they won the second test they were still uncertain. Carwyn James said he was more confident of the Lions' victory after losing the second test than after winning the first.'

For Barry John, the third test encapsulates the '71 Lions experience. And the player famed for his 'Don't worry boys, it's only a game' nonchalance was feeling the heat: 'This was the shoot-out of shoot-outs. We had won the first test, New Zealand came back to win the second; it was win or bust in Wellington. That game was the first time I have felt pressure before a rugby match. It began to dawn on me, as thousands of British fans arrived for the game, just what was being expected of us – and of me in particular.

2001 Lions coach Graham Henry was influenced by 1971 Lions coach Carwyn James

'Our success down under had captured their imagination. My old mate Clem Thomas arrived to tell me, "BJ, you just don't realise how big you are back home. The coverage is making you out like a film star." I just assumed that Clem was exaggerating things, but with every plane that came to New Zealand, there arrived a new influx of Britons. The only thing they wanted to talk about was the big game. I suddenly realised I had to handle this pressure, pull myself together and make sure I didn't bottle it.

'For the first 20 minutes of the match, we played brilliant rugby. Gareth Edwards played as well during that period as at any time in career as we went 13–0 up. After that we were never going to lose. And we made sure we drew the fourth and final test to ensure we left New Zealand with a 2–1 victory under our belts. The tour changed attitudes in Britain towards rugby. It was the first time we had knocked football off the back pages.'

Rugby had indeed become rock n' roll – and Barry John was the Elvis of the oval ball on both sides of the planet. John Reason, author of *The Victorious Lions*, the definitive account of the '71 Tour, captured the Kiwis' bemused view of the fly half's ethereal brilliance: 'They thought of John as a being from another planet'. The game's new-found glamour was all the more remarkable, given the primitive means by which fans followed their heroes' progress from 12,000 miles away. For the supporter reared on live coverage, action replays, gainline graphics and Bill McLaren's magical metaphors, cwtching down with a radio under the blankets in the dead of night does not appeal. But cwtch down they did, listening to word-pictures painting the passages of play between the crackle and hiss. 'I can still remember the agonising tension as the fourth test was played out via transistor,' says Stephen Jones.

Readers of the *Western Mail*, meanwhile, lapped up the copious copy of legendary sports editor J.B.G. Thomas, filling the letters' page with grateful eulogies to the depth and quality of coverage. Schoolboys submitted poems called 'Our Welsh Heroes' while a fulsome editorial entitled 'A nation's pride' suggested 'The title Captain of the Century should be created and bestowed on John Dawes'.

The Lions themselves were largely unaware of the roar they were creating back home. 'Cliff Morgan arrived after the tour had got underway and said "You won't believe the interest there is",' recalls Gerald Davies. 'He told us "People are staying up through the night to listen to the matches, the newspapers are devoting more and more space to reports". We couldn't believe it, but then we were hermetically sealed on tour – we only got to see the New Zealand coverage. It was only when we arrived at Heathrow that we realised the scale of the reaction.'

Five thousand supporters singing '*Sosban Fach*', 'Bread of Heaven' and 'Lloyd George Knew My Father, My Father Knew John Dawes' mobbed the returning rugby tourists. Two lines of fans formed a triumphal arch as the team came off the plane and were tunnelled towards their families. 'The reception at Heathrow was absolutely sensational,' remembers John Taylor, the London Welsh flanker/tour conductor who supplemented his dynamic performances on the pitch with keeping teammates pitch-perfect in their renditions of 'Sloop John B'. 'I had been on the 1968 Lions Tour and there were just two men and the proverbial dog to meet us when we got back. But when we arrived home in '71 we could not believe it. In fact, I thought The Beatles must be arriving at the same time but the thousands were all for us! Brilliant.'

The party didn't end there. The entire population of Gwaun-caegurwen turned out to cheer Gareth Edwards home. A motorcade of 50 cars and a police escort accompanied his vintage car on the 12-mile journey from the station. Bunting strung across the streets greeted the then 24-year-old scrum half as he entered the village, en route to a reception for a 1,000 people in the local hall. Similar scenes of civic pride hailed other Welsh lions home while Carwyn James was met by a welcoming committee that included Plaid Cymru leader Gwynfor Evans and folk icon Dafydd Iwan. The Lions became the first rugby team to enter 10 Downing Street as Edward Heath hosted a reception to celebrate their success and they won Team of the Year at the BBC Sports Personality Awards, rounding off their appearance with a burst of tour song 'Sloop John B'.

Gerald Davies

The legacy of the '71 Tour lives on. John Taylor describes it as the 'massive turning point' that finally banished British rugby's inferiority complex. Gerald Davies agrees: 'Until that point there had been an introversion about British and Irish play. Beating the best team in the world – beating New Zealand in New Zealand – gave you the feeling there was no obstacle that could not be overcome'. It was also the tour that electrified the game's image. 'It gave public and players a taste for Lions Glory which they have yet to lose,' says Stephen Jones. 'Of the last seven tours, the Lions have been victorious in four, after failing in every one in the century previous to 1971.'

And it was the tour that crystallised Graham Henry's coaching ambitions. In providing Henry with the ultimate role model, the spirit of '71 may still be felt when his 21st century Lions begin their quest for glory.

May 2001

Of course, Henry's Lions lost the 2001 series in Australia 2-1. He was vilified by the media even though the series went down to the final line-out of the third test. But Henry had the last laugh when his All Blacks hammered Woodward's 'fittest, best-prepared Lions ever' in 2005.

....

Jack and Bleddyn and the Boys of New Zealand

In the run up to the 2005 Lions Tour to New Zealand I made a series for BBC Radio Wales tracing the part Welshmen had played in the history of the Lions. It was a labour of love as it basically involved chatting to the greats of the game, starting with the wonderful gentlemanly double-act that was Jack and Bleddyn.

'YOU'RE here to see the boys aren't you,' says the clubhouse manager at Cardiff Arms Park. 'I've opened up the Trophy Room for you so you'll have a bit of peace for the interview.'

The 'boys' in question are 85 and 82 respectively but it is entirely appropriate that the Trophy Room is the setting for our chat because Doctor Jack Matthews and Bleddyn Williams are living treasures of world rugby. Their conversational double act is as seamless as their former centre partnership for Wales – Bleddyn is the authoritative straight man while Jack twinkles with mischievous anecdotes.

'Just don't ask him any questions about Clive Woodward,' jokes Bleddyn as we settle in front of the silverware. Jack regards the leviathan that is the modern Lions tour with a mix of amusement and incredulity. But when you were a 1950 Lion who had to buy your own blazer, dinner jacket and pay the wages of a locum to cover your six months' leave, you would view the corporate luxury of the modern player rather differently.

'And what's more, we had to pay £50 as a bond against our behaviour,' adds Bleddyn.

'And I don't remember getting it back!' laughs Jack.

Not that the Welsh centres would have had it any other way. The sacrifices had to be made. 'It wasn't easy for our families,' Bleddyn admits, 'I had a three-year-old child at the time but both our wives said "You must go". It was as simple as that.' So off they went on the SS *Ceramic*, via the Panama Canal, on a five-week journey to the land of the long white cloud. 'It was a marvellous trip. We "bonded" as they would say today, very quickly,' says Bleddyn. 'Graham Budge didn't get out of his bunk for six weeks,' chuckles Jack. 'He would just lie there telling stories.'

Some unlikely friendships were also forged, notably between forward Cliff Davies, a miner from Kenfig Hill and William Jordan, High Commissioner for New Zealand. 'Cliff was a tremendous character. The High Commissioner was going back home after finishing his term in London. And each night he played crib with Cliff Davies. At the end of the journey the High Commissioner said of Cliff, "He's the most remarkable man I've ever met in my life." Cliff was a miner, tremendously well-read, beautiful singing voice. Amazing fellow.'

The 1950 Lions arrived in Wellington to a rapturous welcome. Their expansive, free-flowing style of play also impressed their rugby-mad hosts. The squad contained 13 players from Grand Slam Champions Wales. One more, the 19-year-old Lewis Jones, would join them later, becoming the first Lion to fly in the process. 'We played the sort of rugby the '71 Lions played, we ran the ball every time. We wanted to enjoy ourselves and the New Zealanders loved it,' says Bleddyn. The Lions drew the first test and suffered narrow defeats in the next three, but the tour's success was measured in other ways.

'Great friendships,' they concur. 'And we got to see so much of the country,' adds Bleddyn. 'We travelled everywhere by train. One day I was sitting up front so I could take in the magnificent scenery and there was a woman on the line, flagging down the train. Fair play to the driver, he said "It's a private train, we can stop – take your time". It transpired she'd heard there was a Williams in the Lions party. Her name was Williams too – she was a farmer's wife, originally from Abertillery – and wondered if we were related!' After explaining his family roots were in Chepstow and the Vale of Glamorgan, Bleddyn and the farmer's wife decided their chances of being related were slim. 'But she'd brought me a posy of violets and had walked five miles just to stop the train. Incredible.'

Prince of Centres Bleddyn Williams

Even now, the people of New Zealand cherish their memories of the 1950 Lions. Bleddyn recently had a letter from a 67-year-old, thanking him for a Lions badge he received as a 12-year-old. 'He didn't write at the time but his mother sent me a cake. He was apologising for leaving it 55 years to say thank you himself!' Jack also still gets fan mail: 'I had a letter from someone who was a youngster then and he told me that he still believes the 1950 Lions were the best side to come to his country.' It would seem the boys of New Zealand will never forget the 'the boys' Jack and Bleddyn.

May 28, 2005

A young Jack Matthews

*W*e lost Bleddyn in 2009, the same year as a stroke cruelly robbed Jack of his quality of life. When Jack died in July 2012, I'd like to think Wales's greatest sporting soulmates were reunited

. . . .

Lions caged in Woodward's Time Machine

*T*he disappointment of the 2005 Lions 'Blackwash' was intense. So much
talent, so many duff selections and all that ridiculous spin-doctoring. But
on the morning of the first test there was so much excitement. It lasted all of
90 seconds

ONE of the more traumatic aspects of watching the Lions being declawed was the unearthly hour of broadcast. At least when you get stuffed in your own time zone you can head for the sorrow-drowning sanctuary of the bar. But breakfast test match defeats leave the whole day to brood, analyse and construct imaginary 'I told you so' show-downs with Sir Clive.

Before kick-off, we weren't sure which was the bigger event – the first time the All Blacks had faced the Lions for 12 years or the fact that all the Hitts managed to drag themselves from bed before 8am on a Saturday morning. Having decided to make it a family affair by watching it at my brother's house, my mother and I could be seen sprinting through Pontrhondda in the early hours with bleary eyes and hair like Phyllis Diller. Mam was so keen to get the best spot on the settee, she jinked up the path, lunged for the milk bottle on the step and knocked it on, smashing glass and semi-skimmed all over the front door. Little did we know then, it was a move the Lions would replicate all morning.

'Great build up,' pinged a text from *Western Mail* deputy editor Ceri Gould, but picking up the shards ensured we missed the stirring opening message, invoking the spirit of '71, from Gerald Davies. The Lions were prowling in the tunnel, Gethin Jenkins inhaling the atmosphere, Ryan Jones as cool as a Glastonbury pop idol and Alistair Campbell, still wearing his ridiculous tracksuit bottoms and unaware he would be spending the rest of the week spinning more furiously than an 18th-century weaver.

O'Driscoll had time for a final interview. 'How quickly are the juices flowing Brian?' Sky Sport's Graham Simmons doesn't half ask stupid questions. Last week he probed: 'What exactly are you smelling now, Clive?' After Woodward's eulogy to the Welsh, we could have told him what we were smelling – a big rat and the aroma of wilting English roses.

Back in the studio, Scott Quinnell had survived the hilarious embarrassment of the previous night when he watched dad Derek admit he was 'pwping himself' when he faced the haka. 'The time for chopsing is over now,' said the Scarlet legend. 'I'm going for the Lions – I haven't come all this way to watch them lose.' In defiant formation, if the Lions were sharing Quinnell Senior's response to the haka, it didn't show. A smiling O'Driscoll picked up a blade of grass to represent the leaf that is laid at the feet of Maori warriors in reply to their war dance. How poignant that image now seems. Within 90 brutal seconds his Lions tour was over.

104

Dwayne Peel battles the All Blacks and the elements during the first test at Christchurch in 2005

Our spirits rose with the appearance of Ryan Jones, who got stuck in faster than you can say: 'should have been there from the start'. Stuart Barnes also approved. The Welsh-raised Englishman loves the fact Ryan shares his Bassaleg roots almost as much as he rates the Osprey's barnstorming style of play.

The Mullet from Leinster, meanwhile, was catching the eye for all the wrong reasons. 'Where's Mefin?' sighed my father as yet another line-out ball from Shane Byrne was scooped up hungrily by the New Zealand locks. At half-time, my five-year-old nephew made his entrance, walked to the television and pointed to the score line. 'Eleven...zero,' he announced. Even someone wearing Bob the Builder pyjamas knew it was all going horribly wrong. His seven-year-old sister was even less impressed. 'That's not very nice, the way they put their noses between each other's bums,' she said disdainfully, as the first scrum of the second half formed. But then she was in a minor poody having been forced to sacrifice that morning's episode of CBBC's *Watch My Chops*.

Watch My Chops could have been a good mantra for the Lions. Communication was a major issue as Woodward's untried combinations unravelled in the hailstones. The playmaking role hovered between Stephen Jones and Wilkinson, with the former, at times, deferring uncomfortably to the Englishman shifted to centre. As the Lions kicked away what scraps of possession they had, it seemed Woodward's game plan was already drawn from his new football job. And while they made heavy weather of the atrocious playing conditions, the All Blacks seemed oblivious to the icy monsoon. 'Imagine how they'll play if it's fine next week,' said my father.

'The Lions are getting swallowed now,' declared Miles Harrison. At the final whistle Graham Henry revealed the satisfied smile of a man replete. His All Blacks had eaten up almost everyone. Before Woodward fronted up with some Campbell-honed soundbites, there was a commercial break. 'Selection nightmare' was the slogan on the Guinness advert. Never was a product placement so appropriate. Ryan Jones diplomatically side-stepped a loaded question on the doomed decision to choose English experience over Welsh form but there will be no escape for Woodward. Our body clocks may have been disrupted by Saturday's early start but the Lions coach should never have allowed his to be stuck in November 2003.

June 27, 2005

Under Sir Clive Woodward the Lions failed to roar in New Zealand

Flying in to the Lair of the Mighty Boks

The 2009 British and Irish Lions Tour was a dazzling mix of beauty and beastliness. South Africa's safari landscapes provided a stunning backdrop to some pretty brutal action on the field. But while the test series was narrowly lost, the tour was a victory for the values of Lions rugby, marking a return to the traditional culture of the game's favourite touring team.

FLIGHT SA221 to Cape Town took off from Heathrow with excited rugby fans from the four corners of these isles filling its rows.

There was the Resolven RFC contingent in natty blue tour T-shirts; a gang of West Country lads with 'Wurzels' written across their shoulders; a few Twickenham types in barbershop-style stripey blazers and plenty of Welsh jerseys stretched across bellies rounded from years of rugby globetrotting.

There were junior fans too, a Northern Irish family with young boys and a couple of tots clinging to their Lions-shirted parents.

And there was me, sitting next to a nice girl called Mandy, who runs the Wasps Supporters Club and spoke in glowing terms about 'Gats, Shaun and Howley' adding, 'this tour is Wasps and Wales really, isn't it?'

As Lions-branded backpacks were stowed, there was a warm welcome from the South African pilot... and the inevitable warning. 'I hope you have a wonderful time in our country but don't forget our mighty Springboks will do very well.' Have you noticed 'Mighty' and 'Springboks' are paired in the vocabulary of rugby as often as Edwards and Bennett? We hadn't even crossed the Channel and they were reminding us of their near mythic status.

The Welsh Lions supporter has awesome strength in another realm, however. He can talk, booze and crack jokes with the kind of intense commitment Victor Matfield applies to stealing opposition line-out ball. There is no sleeping on this tour.

At 2am the blokes behind me were on a chirpy conversational marathon which roamed around subjects as diverse as the structure of youth rugby, the merits of a good Merlot and the appeal of Katherine Jenkins.

I wouldn't have minded, but I was in blanket, flight socks and inflatable travel pillow mode by then and the one who was standing up, yapping and leaning on my seat had me pinned by my hair to it with his elbow.

Having drained South African Airways of every last alcoholic beverage – the beer ran out long before lights out – the late night chat show thankfully switched off before I was scalped. By the time we were catching our first glimpse of Table Mountain, pin sharp against

Even in 2009 the South Africans were still talking about 1974 Lion JPR

(Carolyn Hitt)

the backdrop of a crystal clear Cape Town morning, the bleary-eyed talkers were rather more subdued.

But the buzz began again as the groups retrieved their luggage and went their separate ways, some straight to Durban, the rest of us to the winelands of the Cape to enjoy the landscape and the products of its vineyards before a crack of dawn flight this morning to the venue of the first test.

The hotel chauffeur was keener to talk Lions than Mighty Springboks. 'My father watched the 1974 tour and became obsessed with the British Lions – he collected all these souvenirs, even a blazer. He said they were the best team he'd ever seen,' he explained as we drove past young boys attempting to sell giant sacks of oranges at every crossroads.

'Who was the doctor guy?' he asked. 'Williams?' 'JPR you mean?' 'Yeah, he was amazing. And this time McGeechan has been very clever playing combinations rather than the full test team.' At the hotel and winery, as I gawped at the stunning scenery and anticipated a pleasant hour in the wine-tasting centre, desk manager Dean was expressing his admiration of the '97 Lions.

'They really caught the Springboks out,' he recalled, shaking his head. He wasn't discounting the class of 2009 either. 'I've been impressed with these Lions. Our provincial teams are very strong but the Lions have won every game.' And he reckoned the first test offered the Lions their best chance of replicating the success of 12 years ago.

'The '97 Lions won in Newlands which is quite a neutral venue. Durban has a similar feel, which could work to the Lions' advantage, whereas I wouldn't give them much hope in the hotbed of Loftus Versfeld.'

On the back page of *The Cape Times*, Victor Matfield underlined what it meant to his World Champion team: 'If you're lucky enough to have a Lions Tour during your time with the Springboks, you grab it with both hands,' said the second row colossus. Brian O'Driscoll matched his goosebump-raising rhetoric: 'Defeat is not an option,' he stated.

And with Lions predicted to respond to 'Bok pragmatism' with 'a low-risk approach' it didn't sound as it would be pretty. Just pretty special.

June 20, 2009

. . . .

First Test, Durban – South Africa 26 Lions 21

'YOU are in the kingdom of the Zulu,' came the message over the PA at Durban's ABSA stadium as the chants of 'Lions, Lions, Lions' roared to a climax with minutes to kick-off.

The Welsh fans enjoyed the welcome but they had already made themselves entirely at home in this coastal city overlooking the Indian Ocean. From early morning, thousands of supporters had brought a dash of bright scarlet to the pastel-coloured high rises lining the Durban beach front.

In the foyer of the team hotel, a large Welsh flag hovered over reception as Lions legend Willie John McBride mingled with fans eager for his autograph and match prediction.

An even larger dragon spanned one of the roads leading into the stadium as Resolven RFC formed an unofficial welcoming committee for the hordes heading towards the barbecues and bars.

In the shadow of the stadium stands, 61-year-old Welsh grandmother Alison James was unveiling another dragon with the help of the African dance troupe Amazu Amahle, who would bring an authentic touch to the opening ceremony with their warrior moves.

'Hello Mitchell, Pontllanfraith,' it read. 'It's for my four-month-old grandson,' she explained. 'We waited a long time to have him so he's very special. I'm taking this to all the tests. We're having a wonderful time. We've got Robert Jones on our tour. Great player and good Trebanos boy!'

In the sultry South African winter sunshine – 24 hours before the shortest day – the pre-match festivities were hotting up. Live music, cute hospitality wooden huts, car-boot picnics – the atmosphere was somewhere between Twickenham's West Car Park and Glastonbury.

There were signs of Welsh presence everywhere – Ferndale RFC, Neath RFC, Porthmadog on Tour, the Rose and Crown pub complete with Cardiff City FC badges, John Taylor heading for the press box and Phil Bennett being mobbed in the 'Lions' Den' hospitality enclosure.

Nestled among the jeeps and SUVs of the Springbok fans, a battered old Mercedes was attracting all the attention. Two English fans had bought it out here to follow the Lions on four wheels. And they had certainly pimped their ride, spraying it red and white, adding 'British Lions' on the side, 'Pride and Glory' on the bonnet, Union flags on the wing mirrors and players' signatures all over it.

Two Scots lads used their bare chests as their canvas, painting the Lions shield from neck to belly button. 'We did wonder whether we should rub the blue bit off as there are no Scots in the team, but hey, we're still all Lions fans,' said one, rubbing his left breast.

Nick Evans, 25, from Cardiff had accessorised for the occasion with some African warrior chic. He and his English tour mate added spears, shields and loincloths to their Lions shirts.

. . . .

The opposition were also keen to acknowledge the heritage of their visitors – in rather more mischievous fashion. The Naked Zulu Chef restaurant's dish of the day was 'Welsh Rabbit with Bok Droppings'.

But the Bok fans are the rugby world's best wind-up merchants after all. Some did it with charm. 'Four nations against our small country – how can that be a fair contest,' mused one middle-aged gentleman with the classic Afrikaaner handlebar moustache.

'But I must say the Welsh play beautiful rugby.'

Others were more direct. 'It's going to be a whitewash,' declared Nicholas Pearce, a 22-year-old Durban sales rep. 'It's awesome when the Lions come – and we like Brian O'Driscoll – but we're going to win 3–0.'

As kick-off approached, the Lions fans were definitely winning the decibel contest although the home crowd were making full use of the free flags dispatched to every Bok supporter. The traditional African dancers weaved their magic on the pitch – this time minus Alison and her 'Hello Mitchell Pontllanfraith' banner.

'This is the moment we've waited 12 long years for,' boomed the stadium announcer as tingles crept up both red and green spines.

The teams were on the field. The 2009 Test Series had begun.

Would it be first blood to the Lions? No. Stephen Jones's first penalty attempt failed. Minutes later, the Springboks were on the scoreboard, with an ominously powerful try courtesy of their captain John Smit.

On safari with Mike Phillips's mum Morfydd and dad Trevor *(Carolyn Hitt)*

Then to the dismay of our pocket of support high above the field next to the big screen, the Boks seemed to acquire an extra teammate – and sadly he had the whistle. Four penalties followed, each one accompanied from where I was sitting with a running commentary on the dubious parentage of Bryce Lawrence from the Lions' fans – and gleeful chants of 'You're not singing anymore!' from the Boks supporters.

Half-time arrived, 19–7 and a positively funereal hush had settled on the Red Army. But Tom Croft sparked hope with his first try while his second galvanised both fans and his fellow men. From 26–7 down the Lions clawed their way back into contention.

Our nerves were as raw as the Springbok steak we'd feasted on the night before. By the

• •

time Mike Phillips shot through to score five minutes from the death, we were bursting our lungs. Mike's try was a particular joy for our gang as his lovely parents, Morfydd and Trevor, were on our tour.

As the Lions came within a converted try of victory, the green-and-gold faithful weren't singing anymore but in the end Springbok power cancelled out Lions panache.

A prop called Beast helped prevent what could have been a beautiful win. But in the Land of the Zulu, the Lions showed true warrior spirit to fight their way back. It was enough to give us hope that the Boks are beatable. So before our tour headed off on safari, we hoped these Lions could still make a killing in the Second Test.

June 20, 2009

Second Test, Pretoria – South Africa 28 Lions 25

*T*his was definitely the most brutal yet mesmerising game of rugby I have ever watched. It left five Lions in hospital and the fans nursing the pain of what might have been.

THEY were Lion Hearts from one to 15 but, by the final second of one of the most compelling games in rugby history, ours were broken.

For the previous 80 minutes, they had raced in our chests as we witnessed a pulsating contest that brought the Lions within touching distance of keeping the series alive.

The ground heaved with red shirts and resounded with accents giving voice to the Lions chant from every corner of Britain and Ireland. Behind us four Englishmen had a message for Sky's ebullient commentator Stuart: 'Shut Up Barnes,' joked the slogan on their T-shirts.

In the aisle, a giant leprechaun danced a pre-match jig.

The Boys from Abercarn hoisted their flags, Newport's Brian Davies and Paul Hiscott sported daffodil bonnets while Dave Williams in full dragon costume carried the 'Smash the Boks' banner for Trimsaran. Ex-Ammanford teachers Peter Thomas and Roger Phillips took their seats hoping their former star pupil Shane Williams could make an impact from the bench.

Hand in hand, a frail elderly husband and wife made their way gingerly to their seats,

These English fans had a message for the Sky Sports commentator *(Carolyn Hitt)*

111

friendly arms helping them on their way. 'They're the oldest people on our tour,' explained the couple from Limerick next to us, 'they're almost 90.'

On the pitch, one of the youngest Lions fans was making his entrance – Gerald Davies's seven-year-old grandson Thomas, on proud mascot duty.

We were watching from the corner of Loftus Versfeld's Eastern Stand, almost blinded by Pretoria's winter sunlight. But we were even more dazzled by the way the Lions set out their stall from the whistle, their explosive start a complete reversal of the previous week's hesitancy.

South Africa, however, began with an act of madness from their hulking blond flanker Schalk Burger, who celebrated his 50th cap by almost sticking his finger in the eye of Luke Fitzgerald.

'Let's hope Burger gets his chips,' I told the Munster fans next to us.

The referee obliged with a yellow card, though a red would have been more just.

The Lions clocked up a point for every minute the Springbok talisman was off the field, courtesy of Stephen Jones's boot and a thunderous try from Rob Kearney.

The Lions would never resort to the dangerous stupidity of Burger's opening salvo but the ferocity of their commitment felt like a metaphorical one in the eye for every arrogant South African journo who had predicted the Boks would smash the visitors.

And if there was a moment that symbolised the sharpness of the Lions' claws, it was the first scrum in the 17th minute. As the Boks prepared to lock necks with an all-Welsh front row, the mantra of 'Beast, Beast, Beast' spread through the home fans, in homage to their monster prop Tendai Mtawarira. Yet, for the Lions, the weakness of the first test would become the strength of the second. Adam Jones made his thrust, South Africa popped up and the defending Lions were rewarded with a penalty.

Me and my pal Joanne form a front row with Graham Price in Pretoria

(Carolyn Hitt)

Beware the beauty of the Hair Bear, Beast. Abercrave's mop-topped cult hero had got the Boks by the short and curlies.

It was a performance that had a more vintage prop purring at half-time. Graham Price, who himself had tasted victory at Loftus Versfeld in the final Lions test of 1980, was in confident mood, as he stopped for a chat and got besieged by autograph hunters.

The rest of us were daring to dream, too. The giant Lions shirt unfurled at every game was hoisted over our heads and on the field, every player seemed to be growing in their red jersey.

Ian McGeechan had never lost a second Lions test as a player or a coach – his record could be safe in another 40 minutes.

As a clearly-rattled South Africa squandered two penalty attempts and the Lions extended their lead to 19–8, our delirious giant Leprechaun launched into a routine that would have river-danced Michael Flatley off the stage.

But, within minutes of the second half, the hard ground of Loftus had started to resemble a battlefield of red-shirted casualties. A single brutal passage of play saw our props heading for the touchline, Gethin clutching a bloodied cloth to his broken cheekbone, Adam holding a dislocated shoulder. The uncontested scrums that followed took away a vital weapon from the Lions armoury.

And then the backline started to be wounded in action, Brian O'Driscoll finally succumbing to the battering he had endured all game and Jamie Roberts injuring his wrist.

The centres of excellence were gone, forcing a positional re-shuffling that disjointed the Lions' rhythm. Galvanised by Bryan Habana's sparkling score in the 63rd minute, the Boks took full advantage of the disruption in the Red Army's ranks.

Our Adam Jones got the better of The Beast – Tendai Mtawarira

The TMO would hurt the Lions further, judging Fourie's try in field, while the rest of us screamed 'He's in touch!'

A high tackle on Stephen Jones offered the chance to square the scores with two minutes remaining. A draw would be enough to secure a third test decider. Our nerves were in bits – and Stephen's knee looked barely in one piece. How would he ever kick this most crucial penalty with a hobbling run-up?

'Bokke! Bokke! Bokke!' screamed the South African fans beside us, convinced he would fail. But like a soldier hurling himself over the top of one last trench, Stephen took a perfect shot and hit the target. I turned to the Bok fans and roared a defiant retort.

Yet with 15 seconds left on the clock, they would have the last word. Eschewing touch for a reckless up and under, Ronan O'Gara pursued his kick and careered into the airborne figure of Fourie du Preez.

Lions Man of the Series
Jamie Roberts on the
charge

'Oh Ronan, noooooooo!' groaned the Munster fans beside me, before burying their heads in their hands.

Ronan looked as if he was about to cry. He wasn't the only one – tears were welling up in Irish, English, Scottish and Welsh eyes.

Morne Steyne's 53metre kick curved over the bar and was welcomed by the wail of the full-time siren and the anguish of every Lions fan in Pretoria.

The words of Springbok captain John Smit boomed around the stands: 'We left it to the last minute to win, but we'll enjoy it for the next 12 years.'

The Lions had failed to keep the dream of a series win alive but in the cruellest of defeats they preserved the unique spirit of the team that brings four nations together.

No-one who was there to witness two tests against the world champions that went thrillingly to the wire will question the concept of the Lions.

They certainly have a future.

June 27, 2009

Third Test Johannesburg – South Africa 9 Lions 28

COULD have won the first test, should have won the second and thrashed them in the third. For the thousands of Lions fans heading home after their South African adventure there was the consolation of the sweetest of send-offs.

After the agony of those last-gasp defeats, the Lions brought ecstasy to the scarlet-saturated stands of Ellis Park. And for the Welsh divisions of the Red Army there was particular joy that the dancing feet of Shane Williams, the deft hands of Martyn Williams, the crunching tackles of Stephen Jones and the fire of Mike Phillips contributed massively to the tourists' win, matching the biggest ever winning margin against the Springboks.

In supporting terms, the Welsh influence was also crucial once more. Bumping into JPR in the open-air bar before the game, the fullback legend was astounded by the number of Taffs in town. 'They must make up at least 60 per cent,' he said, between being mobbed for photo requests.

JPR had brought a relic of his own Lions career on tour – his 1974 blazer, which despite its snug 1970s tailoring just about still fits. There were fans paying sartorial homage to his rugby generation too. 'Have you seen the Willie John McBrides?' laughed JPR's wife Scilla, 'There are about eight of them, complete with headbands and pipes.'

Other supporters had taken their fancy dress cue from more recent events. Seeing the funny side of Springbok coach Peter de Villiers barking 'rugby is not ballet' analogy, a strapping gang of lads arrived in tutus. The 'Shut Up Barnes' boys were also back in force, as was the giant dragon from Trimsaran and Desperate Husbands On Tour. Desperate Husbands in general have been stampeding the African knick-knack shops of Sandton's shopping malls this week, panicking whether a painted ostrich egg is a suitable last-minute gift for the missus.

The ladies of Malpas RFC were accessorising female fans by handing out their spare collection of daffodil deely boppers. The musical backdrop to this colourful crowd was provided by the British and Irish Lions Choir, created by Mark Burrows – son of Stuart – and conducted by Millennium Stadium regular Hadyn James.

A rousing chorus of 'Cwm Rhondda' brought a homely touch to the formidable fortress that is Ellis Park, a ground which had not witnessed a Springbok defeat since 2001. Situated in one of the more dangerous areas of Johannesburg,

Mike Phillips was on fire in the final Test

115

Feeding time in the lions' den *(Carolyn Hitt)*

Puns in Pretoria *(Carolyn Hitt)*

Andy Powell in a purple frock at the farewell party *(Carolyn Hitt)*

looking at the dereliction beyond its gates it was hard to believe this stadium had hosted the wondrous events of the 1995 World Cup Final.

Yet once safely inside, its place as the beating heart of Bok rugby was tangible, as psyched-up South African fans swivelled to face the Lions supporters and cheekily gesticulated 3–0 with their fingers.

Their team were also in the mood for symbolic gestures. Every Springbok bicep was strapped with a 'Justice 4' armband – a protest against the two-week ban given to Bakkies Botha for his dangerous charge on Adam Jones. Clumsily handwritten in marker pen, it had a touch of the Blue Peters about it. In our section of the West Lower stand, it prompted several retorts about Schalk Burger which remain unprintable.

The confidence of the Bok faithful contrasted with a certain apprehension in the ranks of the Red Army. How would our injury-ravaged squad respond after the mental and physical battering of the previous Saturday with just pride riding on the result? We needn't have worried. The Lion got his claws into the Springbok and roared as if his very life depended on victory.

As Shane collected a magical flick pass from Flutey to sprint behind the posts for his second try, one of my tour-mates, Steve from North Yorkshire, had an apology. English fans have been among the wonder wing's biggest doubters out here. 'OK, I take it all back,' he grinned, 'Shane is brilliant.'

There were more plaudits ringing through the stands minutes later, as Shane collected a high ball, took it into contact and somehow emerged through the pile up of enormous Bok bodies to zip away like a little ferret. He was back with a scintillating performance that would earn him man of the match.

By the time Ugo Monye poached Wynand Olivier's pass to zoom 70m for his interception try in the 54th minute, the game seemed in the bag. There would be no first whitewash in 118 years for the Boks, whose frustration showed itself in the occasional argy bargy outburst.

But we won the fights too. Martyn Williams may have been chucked around like a rag doll after his dust-up with Heinrich Brussow, but the nonchalant grin from Nugget as he got to his feet, only served to rattle his tetchy opponents even more. We then held our breath when Mike Phillips got into a scuffle – mainly because we've been touring with his mam Morfydd and know how much she fears her boy's fabulous feistiness will send him to the bin. But Spiky Mikey played the situation beautifully, earning a Lions penalty in the process.

As a late tackle on Stephen Jones moments later gave the Lions yet another chance to extend their lead, the Bok supporters were barely audible. They were finally silenced by the TMO in the 75th minute as Odwa Ndungane's feet were judged in touch. The disappointment prompted streams of green shirts to head for the exit before the final whistle, an entire stand of Lions fans waving them on their way.

The final whistle saw the players form a tight circle, a bond between four nations that has been replicated among the thousands of fans who have followed their journey across South Africa.

Paul O'Connell took his men on a circuit of the field which ended in a laughing Stephen Jones booting the ball into the heart of the Red Army. 'I hope people don't misconstrue the lap of honour,' said the captain. 'We are under no illusions we've lost the test series but a lot of people have paid a lot of money to come here and we just wanted to thank them.'

The fans also wanted to thank the players – for giving their all in a test series of exhilarating drama and providing the sweetest of send-offs. Yet bittersweet too. It was the trip of a lifetime for so many of us and we gained wonderful memories, new friends and a particular pride in the Welsh contribution to the 2009 British and Irish Lions tour to South Africa. There's just one souvenir we didn't want to bring home – that tantalising sense of what might have been…

July 6, 2009

The power of four: 2009 Lions coaches (from left to right) Robert Howley, Ian McGeechan, Warren Gatland and Shaun Edwards

Chapter 6

Characters and Controversies

Rugby, as played by the Welsh is not a game. It is a tribal mystery.

Gwyn Thomas

If there is a well-used metaphor for Welsh rugby it is the rollercoaster. It works well. Hitting the heights, depths and occasionally feeling extremely queasy certainly covers the experience of being a Welsh fan. This chapter is devoted to some of the most dramatic twists of the rollercoaster during the Noughties.

Voting in the Regional Revolution

On April 5, 2003 the 239 clubs of the Welsh Rugby Union were asked to vote on the seismic step of replacing the nine top-flight teams with four regional sides. I watched from the gallery.

11am The blazerati gather at Port Talbot Civic Centre for the EGM. The last time I was here it was to report on a pensioners' talent show – the spectacle is not dissimilar this morning. With a touch of theatre, Glanmor Griffiths, David Moffett and Sir Tasker Watkins are seated on the stage flanked by fake burning torches. All that's needed are a few vestal virgins to waft from the wings. Sir Tasker punctuates his address with clever quips – he appears to have been scripted by Noel Coward.

11.03am Sir Tasker attempt to get matters underway but there's a point of order from Blackwood before he's barely drawn breath. Someone's complaining they haven't had time to consider the resolution. 'We've only just had this!' he fumes. 'It was sent out on February 6,' counters Sir Tasker. 'We had it on Friday,' he replies'. 'Where do you live?' says Sir Tasker, with perfect comic timing.

11.10am Glanmor Griffiths outlines the deceptively simple Time For Change Motion which is flashed up on the big screen for added emphasis. Are you for or against region-based rugby – and we're recommending four regions, is the basic message. 'Please give us the ammunition we need to change our game for the good of us all,' pleads Glanmor.

11.16am Here comes the science bit. David Moffett takes the stage to explain the nitty gritty. The flu-ridden troubleshooter has wrenched himself from his sickbed but gives an impressive performance without a hint of doublespeak and lashings of diplomacy. 'We've got to adapt or die,' he declares as he underlines the dire state of the game with a list of

The late Sir Tasker Watkins – wise and witty

120

· ·

record losses in recent years on the big screen. The cons as well as the pros are outlined – including the threat of litigation from Llanelli and Cardiff. But the blazerati are looking increasingly convinced, especially when he gives his argument an emotional edge: 'The fans haven't been at fault. They are the best fans in the world and they've had to put up with these performances. We've got to repay them on and off the field. It's time for change. I'm passionate about it. It's important for Wales, it's important for rugby; it's important for international rugby. We have to be able to beat the big five every time we play them'. The applause approaches rapture.

11.53am The debate opens. In his suit and open-neck shirt, Llanelli's Stuart Gallacher, takes the mic as if he's about to launch into a spot of club singing – but he's here to sing about his club. 'This isn't about regional rugby, this is about money,' he says before arguing about the dubious demographic carve-up of Wales – 'We believe West Wales starts at the Loughor bridge and ends at Fishguard' – and claiming Llanelli is already a viable region.

12.12pm Cardiff's Bob Norster uses humour as his weapon to put forward a similar case for Cardiff, addressing his audience as 'Distinguished guests, ladies and gentlemen, fellow athletes'. Nearing the end of his speech, he says 'I can see you're losing the will to live so I'll be brief. Cardiff and Ponty together is an absolute nonsense. David Moffett said to me this debate will make you show your true colours. I'm unashamedly blue and black. I've also worn the red shirt of Wales and the red shirt of the British Lions and it's in the interest of all three that I say the capital has to be utilised in a much better way than these three regions.'

12.25pm Dudley Lloyd of Cilfynydd cuts to the chase. 'Don't let's sit on it boys. Let's make a decision for the good of rugby not for the good of clubs who oppose regionalisation,' while Mike James of Swansea gives the most lyrical response of the meeting. 'We're proud of our history but rugby was born out of a disregard for tradition when William Web Ellis took the ball and ran. It's time for us to put away childish things and put away our history. It's time for change.' Dai Davies of Newtown RFC pumps up the guilt factor by reminding the clubs of the disregard for North Wales. 'Some had the temerity to compare us with the Australian outback. We wish to play a full and active part in the regionalistion of rugby'.

12.35pm The legendary Morlais Thomas of Gowerton RFC rises to a gale of good humoured laughter – and thankfully makes the shortest speech of his life.

12.40pm A show of hands and, with just seven against, the motion is carried. As a chapter in Welsh rugby history opens, Sir Tasker closes the meeting with characteristic wit: 'Thank you all for coming – Evensong is at 6pm'.

1.00pm The blazerati hit the buffet and Moffett faces the press. 'How will you feel if you're later judged to be the man who destroyed the heritage of the game in Wales?' he's asked. 'I'd like to think my epitaph will say I improved Welsh rugby.'

April 5, 2003

● ●

Goodbye to the Great Redeemer

*H*e started as the Great Redeemer, by the time he left there were grumbles *of False Prophet. But whatever your opinion of the Kiwi coach who led Wales to a run of ten victories, it was never dull while he was here. I've since got to know Graham and his wife Raewyn well. The world cup-winning coach retains a genuine love for Wales. This was my verdict at the time he left midway through the 2002 Six Nations.*

THE Great Redeemer may have handed over the reins to the Great Retriever but at Steve Hansen's first post-match press conference the spectre of Graham Henry still hovered. 'Have you heard from your predecessor?' asked a hack solemnly, avoiding his name in much the same way as a superstitious actor refers to The Scottish Play. Hansen confirmed there had indeed been a voice from beyond the coaching grave. 'Graham rang me straight away,' he said, adding that his fellow Kiwi had been delighted with the passionate, pride-restoring performance that almost snaffled a last-minute victory against France.

A mere nine days after his resignation, it already seemed as if ghostly Graham was as much a part of the Welsh rugby past as Delme's cut-off sleeves. No more quips, pods or jokey jousts with Bob Humphrys. The Blazerati got their scapegoat. He's gone but what will we remember – and what would we rather forget – about the Henry reign?

The Henry Humour: The deadpan delivery of Dave Allen, eyebrows from the Roger Moore School of Limited Facial Expression. Every journalist he ever encountered got a rubbing from his sandpaper-dry wit. Sometimes he was hilarious, sometimes mischievously flippant. An example of the latter: when he selected Arwel Thomas for the first time two years into his reign, the press were agog at this new twist in the Great Welsh Outside Half Saga. With a personal 20-point tally, a display of varied attacking options, great tactical kicking and none of those heart-in-mouth 'Oh what's he doing now?' moments, it seemed the forgotten fly half more than justified his recall. 'I wouldn't get carried away,' said Henry. 'It was an adequate performance.' Ouch. How would he console Arwel if he got upset at being deemed merely 'adequate'? asked the affronted journos. 'I'd give him a big cuddle,' he smirked.

Henry was also king of the one-liners. Who can forget the delightful drama of: 'I'm going to coach Wales – and I'm leaving tonight.'

The Messianic Phase: At the peak of Henry's success Wales got carried away on a tide of religious ecstasy. No biblical metaphor was left unused. The WRU were even accused of blasphemy for the tone of their Great Redeemer marketing campaign. And when the rugby saviour wrote the Gospel according to Graham, Welsh fans snapping up his autobiography were as feverish as a Llanelli chapel congregation in The Great Revival. 'He's like a god,' gushed one at Henry's first book-signing. 'This is madness,' murmured the Kiwi coach as he exited through the rapturous throng.

The Genetic Experiments: Grannygate stretched those tenuous Welsh connections to breaking point as Henry embarked on one of the biggest exercises in genealogical reclamation since the Mormons started scouring the ancestral archives. In Welsh rugby terms, showing your roots used to be what Scott Quinnell did during his bleached barnet phase. But that was before the family trees of the Southern Hemisphere were examined in the hope of finding an open-side flanker whose great-great grandfather once holidayed in Aberavon. The research was about as thorough as the Titanic lifeboat drill, but it wasn't as if Wales was the only nation shopping around. And faced with an infrastructure he could not change he had to resort to quick-fixes.

The Good Times: Henry may have exited stage left after the tragedy of Dublin but let's not forget the 10-act epic of straight victories that, for a time at least, convinced us that Wales was on the brink of another Golden Era. However he's remembered by rugby history – Great Redeemer or False Prophet – in my book he was worth every last penny, eligibility scandal and eyebrow twitch for providing one of the finest moment of my spectating life. Wales v England 32–31, April 11, 1999, is the Graham Henry memory I'll always cherish.

February 2002

Henry and Howley celebrate beating England at Wembly in 1999 – the most memorable win under the Kiwi coach

· ·

Just who is Steve Hansen?

B efore Wales headed Down Under for the 2003 Rugby World Cup I was asked to write an in-depth profile of the coach who was still an enigma to the Welsh rugby public. In perhaps the most revealing interview he ever gave in Wales, I discovered a man who used to skin sheep for a living, who shrugged off a cancer scare and for whom family, not rugby, comes first. And with hindsight, he did more for Wales than we ever realised at the time. Every player I've talked to remembers him positively. In this extract Hansen gives a coruscating view of the tribalism he believed prevented Wales from thriving.

Steve Hansen imposed a regime of tough love on the Welsh team

STEVE Hansen's office is small, windowless and neat. A single framed print of players in a red-jerseyed huddle hangs above an uncluttered desk. Alongside the training drills penned on the whiteboard is a question printed in five-inch letters: 'Are you contributing to the solution or adding to the problem?'

A favourite quote? 'It's one of my own,' he says. The New Zealander punctuates his conversation with similarly direct appeals for positive thinking. From the self-help-book-tinged optimism of 'We need to be strong, stick with the plan and encourage the people within it to grow' to the classic, 'I take the attitude that the glass is half full rather than half empty.'

Even if it is half full, Welsh rugby's glass is the sort of receptacle you'd find on the Borgias' sideboard – chalice-shaped and laced with arsenic. Yet as Hansen continues Wales's Rugby World Cup preparation off the back of 11 losses and a two-match winning streak, he's still happy sipping from it. 'A lot of people talked about it being a poisoned chalice at the time but to me it was a huge challenge and at this moment it still is. I always will look upon this opportunity as the best thing that's ever happened to me.'

Patience doesn't come easily to a nation that has been waiting almost 25 years for a rugby renaissance but that is what Hansen demands. In a torrid month of internationals that saw Wales outclassed by Ireland and garrotted by England's second string, that patience was stretched to its limits. Hansen was seen to feel the heat of the warm-up matches, enduring calls for his resignation and swearing on air when a journalist dared to suggest that fans prefer winning to improved performances. A lively display of youthful promise in defeating Romania and a dogged victory over Scotland helped restore the faith. Significantly, the players defended their coach throughout. His optimism is based on laying long-term foundations rather than quick-fix solutions.

'A lot of people talk about my test coaching record and it's not something that bothers me,' he states. 'If I leave here and we've won five tests well that's fine as long as when we leave we left it better than we found it. And if we've left something that someone has to pick up and grow we'll have done our job. For too long Welsh rugby has papered over the cracks and the building was falling down inside the paper. David Moffet is ripping his part of the building down, we've ripped ours down and more people are buying into it. And I think the slogan, Together Wales In Union is perfect. We're not all together – we'd be kidding ourselves if we were – but finally we've got something we can come together on. And there's a little more transparency and there's a little bit more honesty than there's been here before and there's a whole lot more light at the end of the tunnel.'

Dressed in cream cotton shorts and a lemon shirt, he cuts a far warmer and more relaxed figure than his world-weary and often defensive press-conference persona. If Hansen attended charm school he must have spent most of his time in detention – at least that would be the impression gained if he were judged solely on his dealings with the media. In a memorable television interview it was put to him that he had been spotted with an uncharacteristic facial expression. 'It has been alleged you have smiled this week, how do you plead?' smirked the presenter. 'Not guilty,' Hansen retorted, with a look of bored exasperation.

Yet the second the microphone is switched off or the notebook closed, a transformation takes place. The monotone media voice becomes more animated as a humour drier than sandpaper is revealed. And yes, he does actually smile. I ask him about this metamorphosis. 'When I watch you being interviewed you come over as... extremely... er...' Fumbling for a euphemism for miserable git, Hansen comes to my rescue. 'Dour is the word they usually use,' he laughs. So does he just despise journalists?

'It's not a discomfort with the media. It's just the 20 per cent of the poor journalists

••

or TV people or radio reporters spoil it for the others to the point where you don't trust them. A lot of the players don't trust them either because they do so much harm. When you don't trust somebody, you never show them the true person you are. The ones that I do trust, I show them a different side to me but I think trust is earned and there are a lot of people in the media here who haven't earned it and probably never will because they don't understand.'

There are times when he can't conceal his exasperation with the Welsh rugby psyche. The Jail of Glamorgan furore is a prime example of cold Kiwi logic colliding with Cymric melodrama. Hansen's attempt to create a residential team camp at the Vale of Glamorgan Hotel was seen in some quarters as control-freakery. To him, it was about attitude, discipline and team-bonding. As a player sneaked home for the night, gossip leaked out about the coach applying his Old Bill detective skills. He allegedly rumbled the escapee's alibi of an early morning walk by feeling the heat of his car engine through the bonnet. 'When we stayed at the Vale of Glamorgan and everyone went bloody bananas over it – we only did it for one campaign – I wanted them to learn that you have to make a sacrifice to be here. When they sit their grand-kids on their knee and say 'When I played for Wales, this is what I had to give up'. You compare what the coal-miner who played for Wales said: 'I worked in the pits in the morning, then I walked to the game'. Now that doesn't compare with what these players have been doing. They've got to pass that on – what are you going to give up? I had to give up my family time. And for a bloke to have been here one day and decide that he was just going to do his own thing and then what made it worse, lie about it. If he hadn't lied about it, I would have given him an ear-piece and said get back, but one of our values is honesty and if you're not living the values, go home and have a think about it.'

He accepts that any Welsh coach must be prepared to have his methods analysed in minute detail. 'A Welsh coach certainly has a lot of baggage to deal with, particularly when he's trying to change something. Right at the moment when we're going through so much change it's been very difficult for myself. It gets very personal and if you take the media personally they're going to kill you. I'm lucky enough to have had a lot of success in my coaching and I know that I'm not a bad coach because we're not winning test matches. But I also know how we're going to win them too and the process you have to go through is going to be painful but we need to be strong and stick with the plan and encourage the people within that to grow. It's very difficult for a Welsh coach because of the tribalism. We've been a nation that's put its hand up and said "We don't want to change". We've dragged them kicking and screaming. Now, every day there are more people turning the lights on and seeing this change isn't actually going to be that bad, it's going to be a positive thing.'

The tribalism gets to him most. For him, it is a source of both fascination and incredulity. While he sees the passion for the sport as a 'great tool that should be used for

An enigma to the public perhaps but Hansen was popular with his players

the benefit of the game and the country', his reading of the national psyche suggests he has been damaged by one too many soul-destroying committee meetings with the blazerati. 'What frustrates me the most is the inability of people to accept change. I understand change is frightening and the people who hate change the most are usually the older people because of a lack of understanding. But there are so many people here who are poisoned by the selfish attitude cancer that runs through this nation. It's stopping you from being the country you can be and I don't just mean that from a rugby point of view. It's not a united country from east to west and north to south. It's pockets of different people And the little villages in the west fight with each other and little villages in the valley derive a lot of satisfaction when one of the villages down the road are put under the cosh. And when you look at the history of Wales and the battles that it's been in, it's been beaten by itself rather than been conquered by somebody else. They've spent so much energy fighting each other they've allowed the enemy to slip in and do the business and take them over or win the things they wanted to win. That's still happening in rugby and it's happening in everyday life in Wales. If we could just get rid of that, this could be one of the greatest nations in the world. The people are lovely but they just have an ability to destroy each other rather than the opposition.'

Hansen has barely drawn breath through this verdict. A few seconds of silence elapse as we both allow its implications to sink in. He's right, of course, but at that moment it's as if we're both reduced to our national stereotypes. Hard as Nails New Zealand. And Insecure Drama Queen Wales. Thanks for the psychological analysis, Steve, but could we now talk about our chances of being one of the greatest nations in the world cup. He believes Wales will make the quarter finals and then it's down to mental toughness. 'When you get to that stage – either against England or South Africa – we've got to take the attitude that this is a one-off game and if we do everything we possibly can then we can pull it off. And if we do that and get beaten then, although we've been beaten by a better side, what would be disappointing would be to get to a quarter final situation and then play poorly, because you don't answer any of the questions you want answered.

'Whenever you perform at any sport or even in your working life, if you give it everything you've got and it doesn't work then you can look yourself in the mirror and say "I just wasn't good enough and these are the things I've got to do to be better". But if you don't give it everything then you don't have any answers and that to me would be more frustrating.'

September 9, 2003

As Hansen predicted, Wales met England in the 2003 Rugby World Cup quarter final and gave their all. As he'd always intended to, he left Wales at the end of the 2004 Six Nations and was given a warm send-off by the Millennium Stadium crowd. His parting words summed up the tough love of the Hansen Era: 'My whole purpose was to try and help it change so it wasn't about short-term results and me going away saying "Hey, look at my test record". It was about going away and looking back and saying "Well, I've helped it get better".

The Day the Music died for Rugby's Guitar Man

After the euphoria of Wales's first Grand Slam for 27 years, the departure of Mike Ruddock less than a year later, amid rumours of player power and contractual breakdowns, was a sad day. From the car-crash telly of Alfie's Scrum V *appearance to the vast damage limitation exercise of the WRU's Red Zone Roadshows, it was a torrid time for the national game. While we may never know what really happened, one thing's for certain – Mike Ruddock is a lovely guy. During the week the drama dominated the front pages I wrote this tribute.*

DISCORD in the camp, contract negotiations that hit all the wrong notes and he's gone before the fat lady sings. None of this has been sweet music to Welsh fans' ears. How could this happen to Mike Ruddock, the warm, self-effacing and thoroughly decent man who seemed capable of creating harmony wherever he went? Sometimes quite literally. If there is an episode that epitomises the kind of person Welsh rugby has just lost, it was an impromptu musical evening at the Vale of Glamorgan before the Grand Slam season kicked off.

The rugby media of Wales were being treated by the Welsh team management to a golf day at their Vale of Glamorgan base. After Ceri Sweeney and Gareth Cooper had trounced everyone on the greens, the Badgers & Weasels – Alan Phillips' affectionate term for journalists – joined the coaching team for dinner. As the pudding plates were cleared away, a guitar was produced and Mike began to sing. From a rousing Elvis medley, complete with curling lip, to more mellow renditions of David Gray, Simon and Garfunkel and Van Morrison numbers, it was a very impressive set. We expected nothing less from the man who still occasionally gigged with his group called Mid Life Crisis.

Everyone joined in and choruses of 'American Pie' drifted late into the night. After a scissors was produced from the kitchen, I hacked off the nails of my left hand and borrowed the guitar for a duet with Mike – an anecdote I dined out on for several months. Well, it's not as if Clive Woodward would ever let you croon along with him to The Eagles' greatest hits.

Ruddock's sudden departure shocked the nation

129

· ·

Sporting hacks can be a cynical bunch but we were enjoying the sort of fun that every rugby club is familiar with – beer, song and laughs. After the mind games that characterised press relations in the darker days of the Henry and Hansen eras, this was a cheering change, a return to a more straightforward relationship. And it wasn't just a charm offensive. Ruddock was a coach completely without PR spin.

That October night seemed the start of an exciting journey. A few weeks later Wales came within tantalising reach of beating South Africa and New Zealand. The momentum grew and the breakthrough came on February 5, 2005, with the defeat of England. In the early hours of the Sunday morning after Wales had won their first Grand Slam for 27 years, Mike picked up his guitar once more. As the nation celebrated, the coach who had helped make their dreams come true sat in the foyer of the Vale of Glamorgan hotel with some of his players, strumming, singing and smiling.

Less than a year later, it would seem that even after producing a Grand Slam in glorious style and providing hope of world cup success, the conditions do not exist for Mike to make everyone sing from the same song sheet. The band plays on while the Welsh rugby public wonders who really calls the tune. All we can say to Mike Ruddock is thank you for the music – on and off the pitch.

February 2006

Perhaps we should have known Wales 2007 Rugby World Cup campaign might hit the skids after that warm-up game in Twickenham in which Wales endured a record stuffing by England. It was rugby played in cricket weather but no-one quite expected us to get hit for 62. Yet I was still so certain of progression to the quarter finals that I booked the most expensive rugby weekend of my life. All we had to do was beat Fiji. Wales's final pool game in Nantes, however, would cost Gareth Jenkins dear...

GARETH THOMAS, barefoot and battle-worn after his 100th cap match went down in Welsh rugby history for all the wrong reasons, spoke with unexpected eloquence.

There was no place in a positively funeral press conference for the usual bullish humour of Alfie.

'We've let a nation of passionate rugby people down,' he said, simply and quietly.

At the final whistle, he had resonant words for his team.

The players were scattered individually across the field, crouching, standing, heads bowed, but, united by that same expression of numb shock. Alfie herded them into a huddle as the Fijians embarked on their delirious lap of honour. So what do you say to a Welsh team that has just shattered the dreams of an entire country?

Coach and captain face the press after Wales's devastating exit in the pool stages of RWC 2007

'I told them it can be the most brilliant thing in the world and the most desperate thing in the world to be a Welsh rugby player. We'll take the flak, the world will keep spinning and everyone will still wake up tomorrow. We'll move on.'

But the weariness in Alfie's voice suggested his personal rugby journey had come to the same painful end as Wales's troubled odyssey through this world cup. It added another layer of sadness to the day's surreal events.

We all woke up the next morning and, yes, the world was still spinning, but so were our heads – with Victor Meldrew's mantra.

'I can't believe it,' was the phrase on every Welsh fan's lips as they left the cobbled streets of Nantes behind.

Just how had Wales managed to blow their world cup campaign quite so spectacularly? But it wasn't just about 80 minutes in Stadium Beaujoire on Saturday that left rugby neutrals purring with delight at the romantic drama of it all. The emergency exit door out of the pool stages was ajar throughout the tournament. In three out of their four games Wales gave themselves more mountains to climb than Ranulph Fiennes.

· ·

Gareth Jenkins was asked if he knew why bad starts had been such a constant theme. 'No, is the simple answer,' he replied. We didn't prepare to do that, that's for sure.

When Wales were 25–3 down, the supporters were so familiar with the Lazarus scenario that many weren't even that worried.

Fijian outside half Nicky Little stretched the lead ever larger with his boot but even though Stephen Jones's efforts kept finding the posts there was the sense that Wales would still prevail. After all, we always come back in the second half, don't we?

And we did for a while, scoring three stylish tries in a 19-minute purple patch, including a vintage Shane Williams effort. His dolphin-like dive over the line was so extravagant he almost spilled the ball, but his exuberance seemed like a signal to the crowd to relax. Unfortunately the Welsh players themselves soon appeared to follow suit.

Fiji had been patronised in the build-up to the game as a one-dimensional side who bung the ball about with abandon. Wales's sharper rugby intellect would surely triumph, as they imposed control and structure on the free-flowing Pacific Islanders. But at critical moments in recent games the only evidence of Welsh brains has been on the bellies of supporters' jerseys. Fiji had the nous, the mindset and the overwhelming desire to produce the biggest upset in 20 years of global competition.

Even the most devastated Welsh fan couldn't begrudge them their moment of glory, achieved in such exhilarating fashion. The sight of Nicky Little stretchered back onto the pitch – still attached to a drip – to be embraced by his teammates will become an iconic tournament image. They even won the singing, forming a circle to perform in sweet two-part harmony.

Anyway, many of us will now have to take an interest in the Pacific Islanders.

Certain that Wales would reach the quarter finals, I booked my Marseille sojourn months ago. One of Gareth Jenkins's parting shots as Welsh coach was to describe how he and his team were 'hurting, bleeding, emotionally on the floor.'

Well I'm not too chuffed to have shelled out £799 to watch Fiji v South Africa either. And I'm not the only one.

October 1, 2007

After the debacle of the 2007 Rugby World Cup, the only way was up for the Welsh rugby rollercoaster. After swiftly dispensing with Gareth Jenkins, the WRU looked to New Zealand for salvation once more. It arrived in the shape of Warren Gatland. But given the torrid time Welsh rugby had endured in the previous few years I thought it best to warn the new coach just what he was taking on…

· ·

A Letter of Welcome to Warren Gatland

Dear Warren,

Croeso i Gymru – Land of Song and Three Milllion Selectors.

Congratulations on becoming the 20th man – and third Kiwi – to negotiate the revolving door of Welsh rugby coaching. We're really chuffed to have you and have been encouraged by the vision you have outlined for our national game. We're also impressed by the way you managed to appear on both the sofas of *Wales Tonight* and *Wales Today* in the space of 20 minutes. Not just an example of slick media skills – anyone who can negotiate the Culverhouse Cross roundabout during the Friday night rush hour with that speed is a pretty nifty guy.

After the WRU scoured the world for you on a weekend break to New Zealand, you've been given a job spec that runs to more pages than a Jackie Collins novel, minus the rude bits, of course. But have they told you everything about what comes with the hottest seat in world rugby? Thought not.

So take this letter as the written equivalent of a friendly pair of asbestos pants. Forewarned, forearmed and all that.

The first thing to be aware of is you will become the biggest celebrity in Wales whether you want to or not. It's a no brainer – your only current competition is Rhydian from *X Factor*. Of course we've got some bigger names but they don't come here much. Ioan's in LA and Sir Anthony's only popping home to Margam Park for his 70th.

You'll fill this celeb void quite nicely. The delights that await you include the moulding of your form into a Mini Grogg; immortalisation in verse by Max Boyce, your signed photo on the wall of Giovanni's in Cardiff and eligibility for next year's 50 Sexiest Men in Wales poll.

It doesn't matter that you're not Welsh. In fact it helps. We love Kiwis – as long as they conform to the stereotype of the complete bastard. Because Wales has a disturbing number of males who are umbilically attached to their Mams and can be reduced to gibbering wrecks by the opening bars of 'Calon Lân', we occasionally need a dose of New Zealand dourness. (Until things go pear-shaped and the cry goes out to go native with a passionate Welshman at the helm once more).

So keep that sensitive side under wraps. Your name should be prefixed with the following adjectives at all times: Hard-Nosed; No-Nonsense; Straight-Talking. You will have learned the lesson from your Kiwi predecessors of what not to do. There is a middle ground between the charming media tart route (Henry) and the not smiling in a press conference for two years approach (Hansen).

The fall from Great Redeemer to False Prophet can be brutally swift. Ways to avoid the

Warren Gatland (left) and Sam Warburton
think what might have been at the
2011 Rugby World Cup

descent include avoiding charging extortionate amounts for the honour of your presence at lower division rugby club dinners and getting paid a fortune for writing about your cats in the *Daily Mirror*.

When it comes to media relations in general, after what's happened in recent months, we'll just be happy if you talk to us. And the English press will only ever ask you questions about Gavin Henson anyway. As for telly, developing a routine of comic banter with Bob Humphrys is always useful, and if Gwyn Jones and Jonathan like you, you're made.

People will keep telling you about the perils of Player Power in these parts, not to mention uncleaned showers, the discarding of half empty water bottles and going on the razz between matches. You probably won't have a problem with it. Our boys only seem to try it on with Welsh coaches.

And last but not least, the fans. We know as a New Zealander, you're familiar with the often deranged psyche of the fanatical rugby supporter, but there are people in Wales who make Heather Mills look reserved. We're rugby nuts. Some of us are just nuts. Indeed one poor soul even cut off his nuts – to fulfil a bet he made that Wales would win the Grand Slam in 2005.

Sensibly, you've begun your reign with the assertion that you are not the new Great Redeemer, Rugby Messiah or Miracle Man. We applaud your pragmatism and the cool realism of the neutral observer. But trouble is, since your appointment has been confirmed, some of us are already succumbing to NDS – as in New Dawn Syndrome.

Symptoms include world cup amnesia. We have wiped our memories of that traumatic defeat by Fiji in Nantes. We aren't bothered that we're currently ranked tenth in the world, languishing in the second tier of rugby nations. And who cares that you've got a mere couple of months to prepare for the toughest of Six Nations openers – world cup finalists England, home at HQ, a place we haven't triumphed at since the decade of Bucks Fizz.

But Warren, here comes your real welcome to Wales. This is not so much the land of make believe, as the land where people always believe. And now they will believe you have the supernatural Kiwi powers to work wonders at Twickers and beyond.

So resist the madness. I'd be happy if you can crack the whip of discipline, galvanise the talent that undoubtedly exists into realising its potential and put a wedge in that revolving door for the next four years. And if you do hit a mid-term wobble, beware of meetings with men in blazers in car parks...

Good luck Warren – Wales is behind you.

Yours in sport,

Carolyn Hitt

November 12, 2007

135

Chapter 7

Grand Slam Diaries 2008 and 2012

We have witnessed the arrival of a new generation of Welsh rugby heroes – a group of players who have equalled the success of those great Welsh teams of the past.

Carwyn Jones

Welsh Grand Slams have been like buses in recent times. We wait 27 years for one and then get three in eight years. Not that I'll ever get blasé about the northern hemisphere clean sweep. Each has been a fascinating story with sub-plots galore. In 2008 it was all about ending the 20-year hoodoo at Twickenham. And with a team bruised by world cup failure, led by a new coach who barely had time to unpack, victory at HQ seemed a particularly tall order. But with Adam Jones's mother leading the support how could Wales fail…

Welsh Mam sees off Barbour Man at Twickenham

February 2, 2008 **England 19 Wales 26**

As Twickenham Man stuffed his hands in his Barbour pockets and slouched off into the wintry night, Welsh Mam was determined to stay and enjoy the party. Wearing her Welsh shirt, scarf and lucky daffodil earrings, June Jones – the delightfully bubbly mother of Hair Bear prop Adam – was leading the singing under the HQ stand.

Performing the solo verses of 'Hymns and Arias' while her gang took up the choruses, June punched the air with delight on the old line that had taken new meaning just minutes before: 'Wales defeated England in a fast and open game…'

Further down the concourse, Mair Jenkins, a primary school teacher from Barry had one arm around a large inflatable daffodil and the other around her best friend Enid. 'I can't stop shaking. I just can't believe it,' beamed Mair. 'I just don't know how that turnaround happened.' Enid was pinching her cheeks. 'It feels like my wedding day,' she laughed. 'My face hurts because I've been smiling so much.'

The pair were thrilled that Wales had finally come full circle at the home of English rugby. 'We were here the last time we won 20 years ago – we were stood right in the corner where Hadley scored,' recalled Mair. 'But this is a hundred times better. I thought we were going to lose and all of a sudden we came back from the dead. I

On tour with Rugby Mam extraordinaire June Jones – mother of Adam *(Carolyn Hitt)*

think the subs made a difference, but I would say that because my husband is called Gethin Jenkins and I always get excited when I hear his name!'

'The noise from the Welsh supporters was incredible,' said Enid. 'But fair play, the English fans around us were great, they clapped us at the end.' The ladies had arrived at the stadium that afternoon, confident the curtain could finally come down on 20 years of HQ horror shows. 'We stayed at the team hotel and we saw their preparation,' said Enid mysteriously. 'There was a real buzz there,' added Mair.

Over at Old Deer Park as fans converged on the spiritual home of Wales in London before the game, there had been a similar optimism. From the marquees to the John Dawes Suite of London Welsh, a quiet hope spread through supporters that the Gatland dream team could put some voodoo on the hoodoo. 'I do so look forward to beating the Welsh,' hammed a plummy voice on the Twickenham Special double decker from Richmond but upstairs BBC Wales's Jason Mohammad was looking forward to the opposite outcome. 'I've just got this vibe we can do it,' he said.

Yet inside the chilly realms of Twickenham's newly-extended fortress, the scale of the task suddenly seemed as big as the giant red cross being unfurled across the turf. Intended as a strident symbol of English patriotism, it also made the pitch look like a massive first aid kit – something which would have come in very handy for the next 80 minutes as casualties littered the field of battle.

Welsh pride was certainly wounded in the first 40. England stripped and ripped the ball at the breakdown, while the stylish David Strettle's searing break through the Welsh defence hinted that Ashton's men would be adding panache to their usual power game. The blond wing's departure with a crocked angle brought no respite. His replacement, Lesley 'The Volcano' Vainikolo, the Tongan-New Zealand rugby league convert soon made his presence felt... mainly on Mark Jones's kidneys. The man with the build of a bison and the braids of Bo Derek gathered a pinpoint kick, flattening Jones in the process, and popped the ball up to Toby Flood to canter over the try line. An ominously easy score.

Images of Welsh misfortune were already stacking up – the sight of Jonathan Thomas crashing to the floor after catching Jonny Wilkinson's swinging forearm; Gavin Henson throwing his arms in the air in exasperation as Toby Flood sidestepped his tackle, and the physical mismatch of Mark Jones and the erupting Volcano.

Half-time came and under the blackened sky it seemed Wales were set for another dark day at Twickenham. 'Make some noise and our O2 Angels will fire their cannons at you!' chirped the stadium announcer. But Welsh fans were in no mood for an airborne goody bag, it felt as if we'd already had everything but the kitchen sink thrown at us.

And yet, despite all that English dominance, there was just a 10-point cushion to show for it. There were small mercies to cling to. Hooky's boots were set to metronome mode

James Hook and Gavin
Henson tackle teammate
Lee Byrne after his try at
Twickenham

and Huw Bennett's arm had stopped Paul Sackey grounding a 38th minute try that would have widened the scoreboard. Twickenham Man was feeling pretty cocky, but Welsh Mam wasn't giving up on her boys.

They repaid her faith. A 57th-minute penalty sparked a hopeful chant of 'Wales, Wales'. Gavin Henson galvanised his teammates with a powerful break through England's defence, slipping Wilkinson's tackle as he went. Another penalty chipped away at their lead and prompted a grateful chorus of 'Cwm Rhondda'. England's new wunderkind Danny Cipriani made his debut to rapturous applause. As he waited to gather a wayward pass from Wilkinson, a voice screeched: 'Bury him!' I was embarrassed to hear it was my own… but thrilled when Shanklin duly obliged. Welcome to international rugby, Danny.

England's rose was wilting but James Hook was blooming brilliant with the Barry John-style ghosting that set up a try for Lee Byrne. A flawless conversion levelled the scores.

Delirious 'Hymns and Arias' drowned the groans of Twickenham Man. And just when you dared to dream that 20 years of hurt were about to be healed, Mike Phillips turned hope into reality, finishing off the try that began with his own charge-down.

On the eve of the game, a documentary on the life of Ray Gravell showed a dressing room talk from his mentor Carwyn James, voicing the mantra: 'It's a thinking game'. So often in recent times, mental fragility has cost Wales games they had the talent to win. But in the final minutes of this match, they thought themselves to victory. As England lost their heads, Wales kept theirs and kept play tight, eating up time while the rest of us chewed our nails. With 15 seconds remaining on the clock, England had their final chance to produce a moment of magic but they'd left it far too late. It was sorcery from Wales that made a 20-year hoodoo disappear.

Brian Ashton was ashen-faced. 'I told the players the key was not to feed Wales,' he said. 'We were pretty good at that in the second half. We took all the food out of the cupboard and put it on a plate.' Warren Gatland and his team looked as if they'd enjoyed the feast. 'The win is everything,' said Gatland. 'It's a monkey off the guys' backs and it will create the self-belief we need and the players will now buy in to what we want to do. It gives the Welsh rugby public a feelgood factor and hopefully put some pride back into the jersey and that is important to us.'

Ryan Jones, whose huge personal tackle count demonstrated how much he'd led by example, said the match marked a turning point. 'We've matured as a group. I'm so proud of the boys because they showed real composure and belief.'

And for Shaun Edwards, who lost his younger brother in a car crash four years ago, the victory had a particularly poignant dimension: 'It was a difficult day for my family,' said Edwards. 'It would have been Billy-Joe's 25th birthday but these lads from Wales, with what they did out there, will have put a smile on my mum's face.'

The players themselves, so often grim-faced in a post-England press conference, had smiles on their faces too. Enjoying his return to international rugby after the briefest of farewells, Martyn Williams was speculating how different the day could have been: 'If I hadn't retired I'd have been sitting in The Walkabout now,' he grinned. Besieged by a media scrum, Gavin Henson's mobile rang mid-interview. 'It's the missus,' he explained, before knocking it off and returning to his match analysis.

I told Adam Jones I'd spotted his mother serenading his success. 'Oh God!' he said, looking like an embarrassed teenager. 'There were some crazy scenes at the end. Everyone was really excited. It's a great start to the Six Nations but there's a long way to go.' Yet just like Adam's Mam, this time Wales are certainly on song.

February 4, 2008

···

Wales Refuse to Choke at the Croke

A clinical 30–15 victory over Scotland and a 47–8 trouncing of Italy saw Wales travel to Dublin in search of the Triple Crown. And the fans sampled Six Nations rugby in Croke Park for the first time.

March 8, 2008   Ireland 12 Wales 16

It might have been International Women's Day but the girls from Trebanos were getting in touch with their masculine side. Tucking into a hearty full Irish breakfast in the Kate's Cottage pub, three of them were dressed as Max Boyce.

'Well, Max is a legend, isn't he?' said Katie O'Donnell from under her black curly wig and retro bobble cap. The 26-year-old marketing officer from the University of Glamorgan was leading her first tour party with great attention to detail – rosettes, oversized leeks and flared jeans, customised with dragon inserts sewn in by her mother-in-law.

I thought I'd give the man himself a call to let him know about this act of homage. 'Max, I've just met three girls dressed up as you.'

'Put them on!'

I handed over the mobile amidst much shrieking over the eggs and bacon.

'We're going to do you proud, Max!' declared Katie.

'Typical Trebanos,' he chuckled down the line.

A 25-strong party of women from Aberystwyth were also applying a sense of adventure to the Dublin weekend. In celebration of a tour party member's 40th birthday they had devised a complex series of tasks to be completed before the 48 hours was up. This included the Pegging Experiment. 'Each of us has to attach a clothes peg to at least four men,' they explained. 'Esther's done brilliantly – she pegged Keith Duffy from Boyzone when he wasn't looking.'

The journey to Croke Park proved to be even more of a challenge for some than clipping the coats of Irish pop stars. The Garda were on mischievous form, as map-wielding Welsh fans made their way through the unfamiliar maze of terraced streets in north Dublin. 'Where's the Cusack Stand?' two girls from Cardiff asked the men in uniform. 'Ah it's shut today, ladies,' grinned the Garda.

Max Boyce's female impersonators   *(Carolyn Hitt)*

Adam Jones swapped his ringlets for dreadlocks in Dublin and there was Triple Crowning Glory for Wales

But the home of Gaelic sport suddenly loomed into view. And very impressive it is too, if a little nippy around its upper regions. 'Will someone please shut the door!' squealed a voice to much laughter, as an icy wind swirled around the highest tier of the stands.

In the Hogan stand, the amateur female pundits were out in force – a line of ladies from Abercrave, including Adam Jones's marvellous mam June – were ready to give a forthright and informed running commentary, much to the alarm of the row of Irishmen in front. 'You realise we're going to have to listen to this for the next 80 minutes,' murmured a Munsterman to his mate as one of the Welsh women made a particularly direct comment about English ref Wayne Barnes.

But first there were the presidential preliminaries to get through. If Murrayfield used to be legendary for its hilarious excess of pipers, pyrotechnics and extras from *Braveheart* in its match build-up, Dublin is the home of the pre-match handshake from the lady in the cashmere coat. Once Irish President Mary McAleese had exchanged pleasantries with every rugby player in the northern hemisphere, it was time for the anthem marathon. No wonder the Welsh boys were already disrobing by the last verse of Ireland's choral double whammy. A Daniel O'Donnell concert would take less time.

A burst of riverdancing muzak greeted Ronan O'Gara's first score in the fourth minute. Stephen Jones's failure to equalize was greeted by groans from Welsh fans, yet though it may have looked a sitter there was enough wind circulating around the swaying posts to transport Dorothy to Oz.

The first quarter belonged to the home team, with Ronan O'Gara's boot exploiting the gusts that carried the ball deep into Welsh territory. But the luck of the Irish deserted them in the 23rd minute as Shane Horgan was shunted back from the try line by Mike Phillips at his physical best. Mike Phillips at his physical worst, however, ended a purple patch for Wales with a yellow card. That's the thing about Spikey Mikey, one minute he's saving a try, the next he's probably cost Wales one with a spot of mindless kneeing.

Yet Wales's response to ten minutes with 14 men at pivotal stages in the game reflected just how far this team has come in terms of mental strength. Brains aren't just on the shirt these days. Ryan Jones said later 'maturity and composure' were key factors in Wales's recent progress. They certainly kept their heads – and the ball – in Phillips's absence. Shane enjoyed his cameo at scrum half and by the time the real number nine returned to the field, Wales had bagged another three points and a big psychological advantage.

As the game loosened, Wales's grip on the Triple Crown tightened, even if, apart from Shane's slicing run, so many of their sparkling attacking moves didn't show up on the scoreboard. There was just the sense that Ireland could not offer anything in return apart from touch-kicks, pick and driving and the occasional solo effort from a frustrated back. 'Come on Ireland, this lot couldn't even beat Fiji!' shouted an exasperated fan. It didn't seem the moment to point out Ireland only just scraped past Georgia in a far less entertaining game. For Wales, thankfully the world cup is ancient history. And in a place where they have no history, they made some on Saturday.

Not that it was a relaxing stroll to the Triple Crown. Hooky's sweetly struck penalty only eased the tension slightly. As Eddie O'Sullivan ruefully remarked, there was still a chance that 'Ireland could have nicked it in the last four minutes'. But it would have been grand larceny. As the Irish fans who shook our hands on the whistle said, Wales played all the rugby and deserved to win.

There were some lovely scenes as they circuited the pitch with the trophy. Adam Jones, who has swapped his Hair Bear ringlets for rather meaner Bo Derek braids, spotted his parents in the stand and gave a cheery thumbs up. And judging by the Bacchanalian scenes in Temple Bar on Saturday night, the Grand Slam is already in our grasp.

Ryan Jones was having none of this mad Taffness, however. His contingency plan for surviving the countdown is already in place. 'I'm going to go home, shut the curtains and put the answerphone on,' he said. 'We can't get involved in all that. This championship is not over. There's one more game to go and the guys have got their eyes on the prize.' Haven't we all.

144

• •

Warren Gatland was asked where this victory ranked in the scheme of his career. 'Today was nice,' he smiled. 'Pretty nice, actually.' Ask any of the 20,000 who were there in Dublin to see it and they'll tell you it was very nice indeed.

March 10, 2008

A Grand Slam built on Miraculous Defence

*W*ales played France at home for the Grand Slam decider. Their tournament-clinching 29–12 win marked two significant records. Shane Williams took sole possession of the all-time try scoring lead for Wales with his 41st try. And Wales finished top of the table having conceded just two tries – the tightest ever defence in the history of the Six Nations. The latter was down to the man who puts the scare in tactics – Welsh defence coach Shaun Edwards. But amid the euphoria of Welsh success there was the worry his contract remained un-renewed. The Western Mail *instructed me to write an open letter to persuade him to stay…*

Dear Shaun,

On behalf of the nation, thank you so much. We couldn't have done it without you. Just two tries conceded in five games. A miraculous statistic. Attacking flair has been a Welsh trademark since we won our first Grand Slam in 1908. As we collect our tenth 100 years later, you've made our defence a thing of wonder.

That's what made the difference throughout the tournament and that's what won it for us on Saturday. We rendered that fancy French backline try-less. Not even Vincent Clerc could dance his way through that impenetrable red wall. And we created our own two tries from the strength of our defence, pressurising the French attack into mistakes pounced on so gloriously by Messrs Shane and Martyn Williams.

They know what you've brought to Welsh rugby. The fabulous fear factor for one thing. Asked for the secret of our defensive transformation, Shane revealed: 'It's probably down to the fact that everyone is scared senseless of Shaun.' And he was only half joking!

Martyn has seen more coaching regimes than any other player in this Welsh team and he knows you're the best: 'All the credit for our defensive work goes to Shaun,' said the Magnificent Seven. 'He has made a difference, he has been unbelievable. It is all about mindset and you saw in the first-half against the French when we didn't have the ball, the amount of work we put in.'

Defence guru Shaun
Edwards who helped
ensure Wales conceded
just two tries in the 2008
Grand Slam campaign

You made the press chuckle earlier in the campaign when you said the players were
excited when they didn't have the ball because it meant they could dazzle in defence just
like they shine in attack. We know what you mean now. It is all about the mindset. And the
character shown in building that 'They shall not pass' mentality has been immense.

If you've made them play out of their skins for fear of the verbal consequences, you've
made them laugh too, building harmony in the camp with your rendition of a Drifters
classic. 'I just wanted the team to have a song and "Saturday Night at the Movies" is the only
one I know the words to,' you explained. 'We had just beaten England and everybody was
just sat down in the dressing room. I started singing and everybody just joined in. It has
become a theme for us now. The players did look at me a bit strangely but I believe you have
to celebrate your victories and there isn't a better way than singing a song.'

In just six weeks, you've certainly struck the right chord. These boys will do anything for
you. You understand them. Even the so-called tricky ones. But speak as you find, you said.
You took Gavin Henson, the world cup outcast, and made him your defensive captain of the
backs. All Gavin has ever needed is reassurance and he's had an outstanding Six Nations.
Likewise Mike Phillips, the number nine previously told he would never be number one
choice, has been heroic in defence. They've stretched every sinew to repay your faith. No

wonder, when you bring those bottles of champagne into the dressing room, your personal man of the match award is the only one that matters.

And you understand the Welsh rugby psyche. You connect to the passion, understand the heritage and relate to the intensity because you feel it yourself. In fact, are you sure you're really English?! But just as you've instilled the need to complement our attacking style with defensive steel, you counter our emotiveness with much-needed pragmatism. 'I'm never happy, am I!' you laughed when we basked in our defensive effort – a Six Nations record – and you pointed out Wales had still conceded an interception try.

As grateful players, pundits and public paid homage to you in the characteristic Welsh way – i.e. just stopping short of beatification – you also modestly sidestepped the plaudits. 'I can assure you, I didn't make one tackle in this Six Nations. The credit must go to the players,' you said, describing how you 'couldn't be prouder of the lads.' We couldn't be prouder of them too but we know the difference you've made is crucial to what's just happened and what could unfold in an exciting future.

Yet as the whole nation bounces back to work this morning with a smile on its face, there's just one worry threatening to take the gloss of this glorious Grand Slam – the thought you could leave us. You've admitted that your contract is 'up in the air'. Like Lee Byrne under the high ball, we want to leap up, nail it, gather it in our embrace and make it safe.

There is talk of links to an English coaching role. Tell them they had their chance, Shaun. We knew your worth while they were faffing around with the meagre offer of an England Saxons job. As Warren Gatland quipped ironically, what a compliment that was. You know the talent you're working with here. You're in a country that cares as much as you do. We really appreciate you – we couldn't have had a better start to our relationship. Let's make it long-term.

Like you Shaun, I'm a Catholic, and the Hail Marys are starting now – I'm praying you'll stay. Savour the 'sensational feeling' you described on seeing your boys seal the Grand Slam. We couldn't have done it without you. And if you stick with Wales think how much more we can do *with* you.

Yours in Sport,

Carolyn Hitt.

March 16, 2008

Grand Slam celebrations with Karen Price, J.J. Williams, Rebecca Evans and Jane Williams
(Carolyn Hitt)

• •

Like the glorious 2008 campaign the success of Wales 2012 Grand Slam season hinged on triumphing in a difficult first away match. There was the added incentive of healing the pain of that world cup semi-final. And while a select few were chasing their third Grand Slam, it was a chance for Wales's new generation to come of age. The opening game against Ireland couldn't have been closer or more compelling.

Breathless and Brave in Dublin as World Cup Ghosts laid to Rest

February 5, 2012 **Ireland 21 Wales 23**

After kicking the penalty that won the game for Wales, Leigh Halfpenny gasped through his post-match interview. No wonder the hero of the hour couldn't find any air. When he lined up the ball in the 79th minute of this pulsating Celtic clash, 50,000 of us sucked the cold Dublin night in and held our collective breath.

'It was the hardest kick I've had to take in my life,' admitted Halfpenny. 'Having to deal with the miss against France (at the world cup) was tough, but putting that one over makes it all worthwhile.'

Halfpenny killed his own French ghost with that superb strike. And there were so many haunting echoes of the world cup semi-final that it seemed Wales might suffer a painful sense of déjà vu.

Missed penalties; the loss of their captain and the spectre of a tip tackle turning Welsh hopes upside down once more were the spectres at this feast of spectacular rugby.

But Gatland's young braves survived their 14-men spell, and just as the sin-binned Bradley Davies was returning to the fray, scored the crucial try that set up a nerve-jangling finale. With just a point separating red and green at the death, it was Ireland's turn to feel the sting of the tip-tackle yellow card as Stephen Ferris's dismissal gave Halfpenny the chance to seal victory.

While the final whistle came with a cacophony of Irish boos, the pockets of Welsh support in the Aviva's emerald stands felt their team deserved to edge it. The neutrals agreed. And whether you were a devastated Irish supporter or a delirious Welsh fan, no-one could deny we had witnessed a blockbusting game of rugby in which the lead changed five times.

It was a day in Dublin to quote the Boycean mantra. But those who could say 'I Was There' came in smaller numbers than usual, the combination of cost and a Sunday kick-off a factor for many.

On the eve of the game there was an invasion of a different sort as Brains Brewery cheekily brought their finest Welsh stout to the Land of Guinness, inviting fans and the press

'The hardest kick I've had to take in my life.'
Leigh Halfpenny kicks Wales to victory in Dublin

pack to sample it in a Ballsbridge pub. Judging by the full-throated singing led by former Wales and Lions scrum half Robert Jones, the Welsh Black stuff went down pretty well in Guinness country.

Robert's fine rendition of 'Calon Lân' proved far more entertaining than our first taste of the 2012 Six Nations – watching Scotland v England on the pub screens. The laboured action of the Calcutta Cup match felt like an episode of *Call The Midwife* – a lot of huffing and puffing and still nothing coming out of the Scottish backline no matter how many chances. I shared the breech birth analogy with BBC Wales commentator Gareth Charles. 'Scotland need a Caesarean,' he grinned.

Yesterday morning, those who had safely delivered some of Wales's finest talent in the early 1980s were enjoying the pre-match festivities in the packed foyer of the team hotel – with the usual tinge of maternal anxiety. June Jones and Morfydd Phillips, mothers of Adam and Mike respectively, were nervous but excited.

Team Phillips had another lady who had helped rear the scrum-half into the man of the match-winning physical specimen of today – his former school cook Anne. 'I helped build those muscles – I made sure he had his protein!' she quipped.

A scattering of former internationals were present in the throng, including Wales's most recent ex-player. In civvies and on media duty, Shane Williams still looked younger than half the team he'd left behind. Gareth Edwards was in contemplative mood. 'So many variables,' he said, referring to the changes imposed by Wales's injury list.

But the icon also had faith in those who had stepped into the breech or were ready for their Welsh baptism. 'It's Alex Cuthbert's first game but remember the way Rhys Williams played on his debut here in Ireland,' he recalled. 'And someone like Bradley Davies could have a stormer.'

Gareth had obviously had a premonition of how the big blond lock would thunder away from Wales's first line-out to set up the attack that almost produced Wales's opening try. If he'd predicted Bradley's rather less intelligent move in the last quarter, however, it might have upped the pre-match tension levels that rose when the visiting fans got their first glimpse of the interior of the Aviva Stadium.

From outside, the replacement for the dilapidated but loveable old lady that was Lansdowne Road resembled an alien craft crash-landed in Dublin's poshest suburb. Or even a giant bedpan.

Inside, however, it was far more impressive, with its curvaceous architecture and stunning use of steel and glass. As usual, Ireland gave it the patriotic full monty of presidential introductions; double anthem, band, thumping drums and green flags for every supporter. And as Wales conceded a penalty within 30 seconds, the emerald overload seemed to have served its nerve-fraying purpose.

George North slips a neat pass to send Jonathan Davies on his way to the try line against Ireland

But Wales soon settled into an attacking rhythm, providing more entertainment in 10 minutes than Scotland and England managed in 80 – Bradley's storming moment, Jamie Roberts's attempt to power through and then Ryan Jones just held up over the line. No try. But what a statement of intent.

Six minutes later with almost psychic judgement, the Welsh fans exercised their vocal chords for their first chorus of 'Bread of Heaven', providing the overture to Priestland's classy break and the slip pass that sent Jonathan Davies in at the corner. The conversion hit the post, but with the territory and possession Wales were enjoying surely the scoreboard would start ticking over.

Yet an Irish try just before the break – starring Ulster hooker Rory Best sprinting like a wing – ensured the home team took a 10–5 lead into the half-time dressing room. 'It's the Rocky Road to Dublin,' chirped the stadium announcer as The Dubliners' pounding classic thumped over the Tannoys. But could Wales find a smooth path to victory? Not if Ireland could help it. They made Wales's route to the win as winding as the Ring of Kerry, stretching their lead within minutes of their return with a Sexton penalty. Eight Welsh points had gone begging by the time Priestland missed his next attempt, but when Halfpenny successfully slotted the next penalty from a more forgiving angle, Wales were back in it.

The temperature may have been dropping with the darkening skies, but the match was heating to boiling point as George North galloped through the men in green, slipped a neat pass to Jonathan Davies to send the centre over for his second try. Ireland responded in ferocious style, earning themselves a penalty that took the score to 16–15.

And just when we thought the tension couldn't get any more unbearable, the curse of the tip-tackle returned. Ireland took almost immediate advantage of Wales's depleted defence as Paul O'Connell stole the line-out and rampaged through the midfield. The Irish pack pounded the Welsh line before spreading it wide to send Osprey Tommy Bowe flying over the line.

But Wales had endured too many last-gasp agonies to let this one slip through their grasp. Their power-packed centres zipped the ball to George North who scored in equally muscular fashion. Just one point in it, then three on offer in the last minute of the game. We held our breath... screamed with joy and exhaled a long sigh of relief into the Dublin night.

The words of man of the match Mike Phillips boomed around the stands. 'Great start for us – let's hope we can kick on from here,' said the strapping scrum half. We had to get our breath back first.

February 6, 2012

Scott Steals a March at Twickenham

After seeing off Scotland 27–13 Wales arrived in Twickenham in search of their 20th Triple Crown and, curiously, the chance to beat England in England for the home nations prize for the very first time. Despite Wales's 'favourites' tag it was nowhere near as comfortable a victory as many fans had predicted.

February 25, 2012   **England 12 Wales 19**

Like a Dickensian urchin, Scott Williams picked the lock and stole the game for Wales.

In one of the most delightful acts of larceny ever witnessed in a test match the Scarlets centre ripped the ball from the biggest player in the English team, second-row behemoth Courtney Lawes.

Williams followed it up with an artful grubber kick, the dodging of the stunned English defence and, as he dived across the line, a victory salute reminiscent of another Scott who sealed a famous win against the Old Enemy.

Gatland added a Fagin-esque touch by telling his young super-sub this superb individual try made up for his earlier effort when he failed to send a scoring pass to George North.

But in the 75th minute of a pulsating clash at Fortress Twickenham, Williams's misdemeanour was swiftly erased by his moment of magic. Wales were finally in the lead. Tom Jones's smiling face and applauding hands filled the big screen. Mr Delilah himself shared our joy but the drama wasn't over yet. Could the last play of the game ensure Wales laughed no more? David Strettle flung himself in at the corner for a try that could have drawn the match – albeit with a tricky conversion to complete.

Leigh Halfpenny caught his legs while Jonathan Davies and George North enveloped the English wing turning him on his back as Strettle's right hand desperately attempted to ground the ball.

Wales waited behind the posts, England gathered on the halfway line and Toby Flood nursed the ball on the touchline, ready to add the extras. The crowd roared every replay – home fans believing Strettle's pressure was sufficiently downward; away supporters seeing the millimetres between ball and grass. Three whole minutes passed.

The Welsh fan next to us reassured his girlfriend. 'It's good it's taking so long – there's obviously doubt,' he said before analysing referee Steve Walsh's body language. 'Look how low his hands are... it's... going to be... NO TRY!'

The upper east stand, which seemed to have the biggest Welsh ticket allocation, added screams of celebration to the English boos spreading through HQ. Grown men hugged and high-fived, a couple with matching leek head-dresses kissed and my match companion Ceri thumped my arm so hard I could have done with an ice bath yesterday morning.

In an even more bruising encounter, Wales had finally rewarded the optimism that had been tangible as red shirts filled the sunny streets of Richmond on Saturday.

Despite Wales's favourites' status, HQ had its usual intimidating aura. More Bullingdon Club than rugby club, it's also so much more male than the Millennium. Comedy match outfits – including an entire group of Wizard of Oz characters – were left to the Welsh, although English rugby had a recognisable uniform of its own that can be equally amusing. The tweed and mustard corduroy quota was still high though the navy quilted jacket has replaced the Barbour as the Twickenham garment of choice.

The pre-match was thoroughly old-school too. While the Welsh build-up of pyrotechnics and theatre is reaching *Cirque du Soleil* proportions, Twickenham's only concession to West End razzamatazz was an anthem singer from *Les Mis*.

Her pretty voice was overwhelmed by the testosterone-drenched rendition of the anthems from both teams. As befits this most intense and fundamental of sporting contests, it was full-blooded stuff.

And in the opening 20 minutes it looked as if Wales had drawn most inspiration from those fervent *Gwlads*. As Mike Phillips slipped a beautiful inside pass to send George North thundering towards the line, Wales looked on their way to the best possible start.

Ankle-tapped by Strettle, the teenager bounced back for another assault on the left wing only to be ushered into touch. Yet despite all this Welsh dominance of possession and territory, there was nothing to show for it. After Halfpenny missed the opening penalty in the 19th minute, England were first on the scoreboard.

The match evolved into a more balanced and barnstorming encounter, with neither defence yielding, some brutal hits and only penalties to show for either side's endeavour. There were signs of Welsh edginess too; Priestland in particular seemed out of sorts.

When he was yellow-carded early in the second half, uncomfortable memories of another Welsh sin-binning at Twickenham returned. But Wales weren't going to concede 17 points this time. Indeed by the time Priestland was back on the pitch they had gained three, Halfpenny adding to his immense defensive performance with a consistent boot.

England's baby-faced fly half had shone throughout the tournament with the maturity of his composed kicking. But when the chance came for Owen Farrell to stretch the lead from 12–9 he tugged it wide. A less than fatherly expression spread across the face of his dad and coach Andy.

It could have been the turning point for the men in white, but it fell to Scott Williams, and a try that will rank as one of the finest in Six Nations history, to provide the game-changing brilliance and a 20th Triple Crown for Wales.

As captain Sam climbed into the stand to collect the trophy and embraces from every WRU committee member, the players showed delight yet dignity in their celebrations. Their leader's voice over the Tannoy told the crowds Wales had won the 'toughest game of the Six Nations' without playing 'at all well'.

No matter. We've witnessed too many games where Wales have played wonderfully and lost to care that this hard-fought victory was less than perfect. The result certainly was.

And the Slam was on.

February 27, 2012

The cheekiest of individual tries at Twickers from match-winner Scott Williams

· ·

The prospect of Grand Slam glory was overshadowed on the eve of the deciding match with France by the death of Mervyn Davies. But if any inspiration were needed for Warburton's generation could there be anything better than the example set by Wales's greatest ever Grand Slam captain.

March 17, 2012   **Wales 16 France 9**

It began with poignant silence to honour a past hero. It ended with euphoric noise to salute a Welsh team of future icons.

No wonder Gerald Davies wiped away a tear on the final whistle. 'It was a mixture of emotions,' he admitted. 'There was joy at this young side getting the Grand Slam they so richly deserve – they showed the world cup was no fluke and they have been the best team throughout this tournament. But there was also sadness for Mervyn. It reminded us of a journey we'd all taken so many years ago.'

Contemplating the journey ahead of these youthful conquerors of the northern hemisphere gave our celebrations an added edge. Wales's 11th Grand Slam – the third in eight years – is built on firm foundations and the promise of so much more to come.

They achieved it in a game that was dogged rather than dazzling, brutal rather than beautiful. They put their bodies on the line and kept their minds focused on the prize amid the madness of a quarter of a million fans creating good-humoured carnage across Cardiff, and thousands more glued to screens in clubs, pubs and living rooms across Wales.

The streets of the capital were a riot of colour and carousing in the countdown to kick-off. The French were here in force from the gang dressed as Provençal butchers singing folk songs in the Hayes to teenagers with tricoloured faces in St Mary Street. But Wales could boast the furthest travelled support. They crossed the Atlantic as well as the Severn. Expats Shan and Rob Gravell – originally from Brynmawr – flew in from Detroit on Friday especially for the match. 'Once they beat England we thought the Grand Slam would be on,' said Shan describing their decision to book $1,000 flights. 'We um-med and ah-ed but we thought "You're only young once".'

And some Welsh fans were very young indeed, including a babe in arms in red jersey and ear-protectors. On the pavement outside Gate 5, Huw Jones from Blackwood was patiently helping his daughter Sophie dress in full Welsh costume. The youngster's age spanned Wales's recent Grand Slam years.

'She was born in 2005. She was too young to watch 2008 but today she's going to see her first Grand Slam,' he grinned as Sophie added that it was her idea to dress patriotically for the occasion.

On the big screen in front of St David's Hall the lacklustre Wooden Spoon decider from Rome was on. But a message came that the Welsh game would not be shown as the Hayes couldn't take the crush. Not that anyone minded – the big screen in Cathays Park had room for 10,000.

By the time the Welsh team coach was ploughing through the throng, the crowd was positively biblical. For the players it was an inspirational sight, Gatland said later. He also revealed there was a motivational scene unfolding inside the coach.

During the build-up to the French clash Wales had played down the notion of revenge for the heartbreak of the world cup semi. But as the team approached the Millennium Stadium a 30-second clip of that game was shown to the players. 'We just wanted to show the guys a reminder of that day,' said Gatland. 'No-one talked about wanting revenge – but it was extra special to win after what happened in New Zealand.'

To the pictures the Welsh coach added a few rousing words: 'Make a nation proud.'

But first the nation wanted to show its pride in the team which has given them so much to savour in recent weeks. Crammed with 74,178 spectators – including Tom Jones and Barry Mason, the man who penned 'Delilah' – the stadium resounded to the roar that accompanied the first Welshman on to the pitch, Matthew Rees leading his teammates out on his 50th cap.

In silence pierced by a ripple of applause, they also showed their pride in Mervyn Davies as his image was displayed on the giant screens. Judging by the fervour with which Wales ripped into France in the first minutes the spirit of the Grand Slam captain was there too.

But despite ferocious endeavour from the men in red, Les Blues claimed the opening points with a penalty from the boot of Yachvili. When Priestland's attempt to equalise a few minutes later hit the post, a slight unease spread through the stands. No-one wanted the déjà vu of the kicking problems Wales suffered in their last meeting with France.

But the fly half – who had more than rediscovered his mojo for this game – wasn't rattled while the frazzled nerves of the fans were soothed in spectacular fashion in the 22nd minute. It started with Welsh tackling machine Dan Lydiate almost sending Thierry Dusautoir back to Paris with the force of his hit.

Alun Wyn Jones snaffled the ball the French flanker coughed up and it was spread to Alex Cuthbert who carved his way through defenders for an exhilarating try. At the start of the season the horse-riding wing wondered if he would make the Blues squad. By the end of the Six Nations he had galloped into rugby history with the only try of the Grand Slam decider.

Half-time arrived with Wales extending their lead to 10–3. During the break it was the fans' turn to perform, lending their vocals to Paul Child's jazzy rendition of 'Cwm Rhondda', ready for CD release on the final whistle if Wales won.

• •

But it was France who seemed suddenly on song. While their rather portly number 10, Beauxis, did little to spark their backline, the arrival of starlet sub Buttin at fullback galvanised French hopes with his gliding running. Within four minutes of the second half, a Beauxis penalty brought his team within four points of Wales.

His clumsy drop goal attempt wasn't quite so impressive but as Cuthbert reeled from a collision that left him clutching his crown jewels and the crowd adding an empathetic 'ouch', France looked capable of inflicting another kind of pain.

Memories of the world cup semi returned as Leigh Halfpenny lined up a 52nd minute penalty in almost exactly the same position as the kick that fell short. But this time the full-back who has been one of the players of the tournament hoofed it through the posts with room to spare.

The crowd screamed their approval, sensing France were there for the taking. Yet rather than building on their lead, Wales sat on it for a strange, static period of picking and going.

The unease returned.

Rugby's equestrian Alex Cuthbert galloping towards a Grand Slam

By the time France broke free and were making a thundering assault on the Welsh line, unease turned into blind panic. In the stands, that is. On the field Wales kept their nerve with Jonathan Davies securing a try-stopping turnover that left French coach Phillipe Saint-Andre stamping his foot in frustration, and a desperate lunge for the ball from the indomitable Ryan Jones.

But then Wales had to survive a scrum five. After the Welsh pack illegally wheeled it, France opted for a penalty rather than another try attempt. With the score at 13–9 and seven minutes remaining we didn't know whether it was a consolation or not. There was certainly time for Les Blues to spoil the party.

Up in the coaches' box the tension was taking its toll. 'I needed a wee,' Gatland later told laughing reporters. 'But when I got to the gents there was a huge queue so I was worried I wouldn't get back in time.' Note to Welsh fans. Next time the Welsh coach needs a quick comfort break in the dying minutes of a Grand Slam decider put him to the front of the queue, will you? But relief of a different kind came in the form of the matchsealing Halfpenny penalty in the 75th minute, gifted by the petulance of Trinh-Duc who hurled the ball into touch to prevent a quick line-out for Wales.

Frustrated France were going backwards – marched another 10 metres for agitating referee Craig Joubert – and Gatland's young warriors were advancing into Welsh rugby history. By the 78th minute the crowd was on its feet, already celebrating.

The roar spread through the stadium like an audio Mexican Wave, building to a euphoric climax with the moment Ryan Jones instructed Priestland to send the ball into the stand and the hopes for the future of this brilliant young team into the stratosphere.

And at the beginning of a new era, Wales's young heroes dedicated their Grand Slam to Mervyn, the icon of rugby's previous golden age. 'He was a legend of the game and our thoughts go out to his family,' man of the match Dan Lydiate told the cheering thousands. 'This one's for him.'

March 17, 2012

The three successful Six Nations campaigns spanning eight seasons are intriguingly different – from both the players' and fans' perspective.

Having waited 27 years for the 2005 Grand Slam, nothing less than mass hysteria would do. The raw emotion of the Ruddock year was replaced by delighted surprise in 2008 as Gatland began his reign by wrenching Wales from the despair of their world cup debacle.

But with the 2012 Grand Slam came the feeling that this is exactly how it should be for Wales.

Chapter 8

The Incredible Journey – Rugby World Cup 2011

Oh Cymru, that was a valiant defeat. The sporting gods exist to be cruel.

The Sunday Times Editorial

• •

*W*ales's remarkable world cup journey made everyone want to jump on our Cymric bandwagon. Y Ddraig Goch *flew over Downing Street while* The Observer *told its readers 'We're all Welsh now'. And even England fans – fed up of the dwarf-throwing antics of their own team – wished us all the best. But our players didn't just ensure the dragon roared at Number 10. By making the world want to be Welsh, they flew the flag from one to 15. It all began with a nerve-jangling encounter with the defending World Champions.*

September 11, 2011 **South Africa 17 Wales 16**

In the cruel cauldron of the Rugby World Cup a team will of course take an ugly win over a beautiful loss every time.

A weekend of breakfast rugby saw England sending us back to sleep with a turgid and error-strewn display in which not even Saint Jonny could kick a penalty. But nevertheless they ended on the right side of the scoreboard.

By contrast, we woke up to a Welsh performance that pulsated with more nerve-jangling energy than a gallon of espresso. And it may yet cause us a few sleepless nights as we ponder what might have been.

There is nothing more agonising than a defeat that follows a match in which every Welsh sinew has been stretched for the cause. We couldn't have asked more from Gatland's youthful side as they took the game to the defending world champions with a ferocity that was a joy to witness. We could have asked more from the referee, however.

As any Kiwi will tell you, Wayne Barnes has form on causing world cup heartbreak with a controversial decision. Were we robbed on that first half penalty? Hook's kick looked initially wide but then seemed to curve inside the posts. His positive body language showed he thought he'd nailed it. Oh well. It's about time we had something new to angst about since Andy Haden's 1978 line-out dive.

But just as Wales weren't fazed by South Africa scoring within three minutes of kick-off – as Frans Steyn pawed off Shane and ploughed through Hook – so they shrugged off any apparent injustice, kept their composure and got stuck in once more.

I was watching the game in the heart of Scarlet country – at Stephen Jones and Dwayne Peel's Llanelli restaurant, Sosban. And in a brunch-time gathering of around 70 people that included Peel himself, Phil Bennett, Dafydd Jones and Rupert Moon, all eyes were focused on the local boy at number 10.

'Everyone here either knows Rhys Priestland or is related to him,' smiled Sosban restaurateur Simon Wight. You could certainly feel the love. The diners roared their approval as Priestland's intelligent kicking pinned the Boks back in their own 22.

Calm and controlled, Rhys Priestland
steps inside Victor Matfield's tackle

• •

Half-time arrived with Wales very much in the game.

A fly half of a different vintage who knows a thing or two about putting South Africa on the rack, was full of praise.

'This is the most massive game of his life yet he's calm, controlled and has shown variety in his game with some really nice touches,' said Phil Bennett.

Wales as a whole had shown some really nice touches, playing most of the rugby in the first 40 minutes, a spectacle that was visible everywhere apart from the scoreboard. Within minutes of their return a fabulous Welsh phase of attack ended just metres from the try line with Faletau fumbling a poor pass. The opportunity may have come to nothing but the momentum was with the men in red, the departure of South Africa's towering talisman Victor Matfield an added bonus.

Welsh banners from the travelling faithful fluttered in the swirling Wellington wind. Yet it wasn't just the likes of Clwb Rygbi Llangollen making their presence felt. The Welsh squad had their personal cheerleader in the frenetic form of sub Andy Powell, screaming his big blond head off on the touchline.

And there was so much to shout about – Dan Lydiate and Sam Warburton at their dynamic best at the breakdown, and Jamie Roberts replicating how he played against the Boks in a Lions shirt as he powered through the gainline. By time Hook landed the penalty that took Wales to within a point, the world champions were starting to look as scrambled as the egg on our breakfast plates.

To the delight of the Sosban diners, Priestland served the starters to Toby Faletau's main course, first gaining territory with a superb kick into South Africa's 22, then providing the deft inside ball that sent the young Number 8 over the line. The latter may have trimmed his Afro for his world cup debut but judging from the way he thundered to his first tournament try, the haircut has had a reverse Samson effect.

Wales had a 16–10 lead and Faletau was on the charge again, combining with Jamie Roberts on another assault on the South African line. A knock-on halted the attack agonisingly close to the whitewash. When the Boks finally got their chance to reply to this period of Welsh dominance – as replacement wing Francois Hougaard took Du Preez's pass to slip untouched under the posts – they did so ruthlessly.

Opportunities taken. Opportunities squandered. Ultimately this was the difference between the two teams. Two more chances presented themselves for Wales to snatch only their second victory over the Boks in more than a hundred years. Priestland missed a kickable drop goal while Hook's more challenging penalty drifted wide.

Luke Charteris refuels against the Springboks

Back in Sosban, there was huge disappointment mixed with pride. Actor Julian Lewis Jones, who spent several months in South Africa for his role as Nelson Mandela's bodyguard in the Clint Eastwood film *Invictus*, said his phone was buzzing with texts from the rainbow nation.

'I've had loads of messages from friends in South Africa and they all say the same thing – the best team lost,' he said.

'I'm absolutely gutted. This game shows we've come on massively. Our young players showed fantastic mental strength. They were out there with the world's best and took the game to them. It's just that experience won the Boks the game in the end. We played the better rugby but just weren't clinical enough when it mattered. We had them on the ropes and a more seasoned boxer would have put them away. South Africa had two chances and took them. But we should be proud of the way we fronted up physically. And I really feel there are great things to come from this Welsh team.'

Dwayne Peel agreed the mindset of the side could not be faulted.

'Let's not get into the usual debate about whether Wales are mentally strong enough to win these close games. At the end this came down to two missed kicks,' said the scrum half.

An 'emotionally exhausted' Rupert Moon said he was proud – particularly of 'Charteris, the unsung hero of the set piece' – but also frustrated.

'The opportunities were there to be taken,' he sighed. 'And it's only going to get harder from here on in. Wales have got to prepare for the Samoan wall that's going to hit them in Hamilton – which will feel like a home game for Samoa with the level of support they'll get there.'

Phil Bennett, who spoke with characteristic passion after the final whistle, shone with admiration for the character Wales had shown: 'People in Wales wondered why Gatland bothered taking the players to Poland – it's as cold in Aber-porth, they joked.

'But those hard weeks have paid off. Those guys were willing to die for him. I've got such pride in that performance. The players gave their all for Wales. The back row was awesome. People said Dan Lydiate gave two penalties away but that man bled for Wales.

'Faletau was epic – a young boy who was playing for Ebbw Vale not so long ago charging at the world champions. And in the second half Sam Warburton became a legend.

'It was a tribute to him when South Africa tried to take him out – they could see what he was doing. He grew as a man in that game.'

But Bennett conceded however small the margin of defeat, the loss now brings a huge burden of pressure. 'We thought this was the big one but having lost against South Africa, Samoa becomes the biggest game of all.'

September 12, 2011

Matching the Samoans' rib-crunching
physicality: Jamie Roberts

. . . .

Samoan Stress on the Settee for the Pyjama Army

As Warburton's young guns took the field for their must-win contest against Samoa, a pyjama army of fans rose in the middle of the night hoping their early start wouldn't be matched by an early world cup exit for Wales.

September 18, 2011   **Wales 17 Samoa 10**

'Real fans don't do Sky+,' declared a rugby-mad friend of mine as the nation decided whether to record while they slept or rise at 4am for the live broadcast of Wales's crucial world cup clash with Samoa.

Those of us who went for the hardcore, early-hours option took various routes to rugby insomnia. Party animals treated it as a very late night; more sensible souls got some shut-eye and set the alarm.

I snoozed on my parents' settee under the duvet from 1am with the telly burbling ITV's interactive shopping programme in the corner.

By the time I surfaced three hours later to the sound of 'World in Union', I'd managed to miss an entire film starring Rutger Hauer as a psychopathic hitchhiker, which was probably just as well.

A Samoa match can often bring horrors of its own.

A quick shout up the stairs to rouse my father from his slumber and the night shift had begun. Across Wales, rugby fans were coming downstairs in their pyjamas like hyperactive kids rising before dawn on Christmas morning.

But Santa was rather late delivering a gift-wrapped victory. I don't think I've ever endured such stress wearing nightwear.

Dan Lydiate's early departure contributed to my nervous breakdown, as Samoa helped themselves to alarming amounts of turnover ball.

If Wales had embraced the South African challenge with the ferocious bite of the underdog, they faced Samoa with the anxiety of favourites fearing their world cup could be over in 80 minutes. Uncharacteristic errors betrayed their edginess.

Not that they shirked the challenge of matching the Polynesians' rib-crunching physicality. Future doctor Jamie Roberts certainly gave Seilala Mapusua a taste of his own medicine when he clattered him into next week, while George North also relished making red on blue contact.

But it was Samoan pressure that brought the opening first half points.

Not content to simply bung the ball with abandon like Pacific Island teams of old, Samoa built patient momentum through almost 20 phases to earn the reward of a try from

167

prop Anthony Pernise. As fullback Paul Williams added the conversion, no-one could dispute that Samoa deserved their 10–6 lead at the break.

On his Hamilton home patch, Warren Gatland had just celebrated his 48th birthday. The 40 minutes he had just endured must have added a few more years.

On the other side of the world an uneasy sense of déjà vu was spreading through a dark Welsh morning. Surely the Samoan world cup jinx could not strike a third time?

Within three minutes of re-emerging from the tunnel, Wales had a chance to close the gap. In keeping with the feverish atmosphere, Rhys Priestland's penalty took a suitably dramatic route over the posts via the crossbar.

The absence of James Hook – nursing an injured shoulder – seemed another setback sent to fray Welsh nerves. But in the 65th minute, his replacement would prove the catalyst for the try that kept Wales in this world cup.

Surviving a challenge that almost took his head off, Leigh Halfpenny escaped from a smothering of blue muscle, checked his head was still there with a tap of his scrum-cap and scarpered down the touchline.

With the try line in tantalising reach, he passed to Jonathan Davies who returned it clumsily. But thankfully Shane too had been in pursuit, scooping up the loose ball and crossing for arguably the most crucial try of his prolific career.

Not that Wales were out of sight. The pyjama army were on the edge of their settees as Samoa took a questionable decision to go for touch rather than take the penalty points with five minutes left on the clock.

And just as we thought Wales would pick and drive their way through the final 10 seconds and hoof the ball safely into the heart of Hamilton's adopted Welsh fan-base, Samoa snaffled it for one last assault.

But the valiant defensive red line that characterised Wales's second half performance stood firm in the face of flying blue bodies.

Wales had finally beaten Samoa in a world cup, easing their path to the knockout stages. It wasn't pretty, but we've had enough beautiful losses to enjoy a thoroughly ugly win.

The light was now seeping through the curtains. Stay up to discover if dwarf-throwing had made a difference to England's passing skills? Or go back to bed dreaming of the intriguing prospect of a possible Wales v Ireland quarter-final?

No contest.

Zzzzzzzzzzzz.

September 19, 2011

No Quarter given as Wales reach the Final Four

Wales's world cup journey was back on the road. The highlight of their 81–7 smashing of tournament minnows Namibia was the moment Gethin Jenkins became Barry John. Such was the virtuoso quality of his try against Namibia, Gethin wasn't so much piano pusher turned piano player as piano pusher turned Artur Rubinstein. Wales's prop idol collected the ball off his toes, palmed off one defender, shimmied past another and burst 30 metres towards the line taking half the Namibian defence over with him. Best front row try since Pricey in Paris 36 years ago.

And when we asked them to kill the ghost of Fiji and we got all-out annihilation in a nine-try extravaganza of skill and sparkle. George North and Jamie Roberts in particular ran riot as the nemesis of Nantes was rendered pointless. As Ireland turned the world cup on its head by defeating Australia to top their pool, the dream of a Six Nations route to the final suddenly seemed a delicious reality.

October 8, 2011 **Wales 22 Ireland 10**

Last four standing and it was Wales who were the stand-out team of the world cup quarter-finals.

Australia scraped into the semis despite their maverick fly half Quade Cooper having a shocker; France finally turned up to put England on the plane, and even the All Blacks looked mortal against the passionate Pumas. But the side who thrilled fans and neutrals alike with the rugby and attitude that was the talk of the tournament was Wales.

Oh, to have been a Welsh fan in Wellington after Gatland's young dragons breathed fire over Ireland's old warriors. Back on this side of the world we were getting used to celebrating over a full Welsh breakfast. Those who lined the Cake Tin with choruses of 'Delilah' had a New Zealand night to remember.

Gareth Thomas revealed to his fellow pundits that he'd joined the party in the team hotel. But the former Welsh captain would have been the only one nursing a hangover yesterday morning.

Alfie's 2011 counterpart didn't even have a drink after leading his team to arguably the most crucial victory in 130 years of Welsh rugby. As we discovered on Twitter, Sam Warburton's idea of post-match hedonism is sharing a chocolate bar with Ryan Bevington.

The last time Wales reached a world cup semi-final the players embarked on a two-day bender that would make the infamous Cardiff binge-drinkers of St Mary Street blush. But the modern players who were a match away from the World Cup Final were content to confine champagne rugby to the pitch.

And how they fizzed in the quarter-final. We used to despair of a Welsh side that kept their best till last, playing 70 minutes of catch-up before a desperate final flourish. This team set out their stall from the start.

Blitzing Ireland from the whistle their reward came within three minutes. Building phases from a won turnover, Toby Faletau almost powered over but was halted just short of the line. The ball was recycled and spread through the Welsh backline to find father of the squad Shane Williams, who squeezed in at the corner. Priestland's confident conversion crowned the perfect start for Wales.

Ireland had their first-half chances but were either denied by heroic Welsh defence or their curious decision to opt for touch rather than three straightforward shots between the posts. Luke Charteris, in particular, notched up a phenomenal tackle count while Shane was at his gymnastic best burrowing under Sean O'Brien to forbid him his touchdown.

Ireland finally made the scoreboard on the half hour with an easy penalty. Halfpenny, on form at fullback, stretched the Welsh lead to 10–3 with a kick from the halfway line.

At the break, we dissected the action over the bacon and eggs in Cardiff's packed Conway pub. It was compelling, brutal and intense rugby and it still felt anyone's game. Would this finally be the moment in Wales's campaign where their opponents' greater experience edged the contest?

As Keith Earls levelled the scores with a try within five minutes of their return, Ireland seemed to have provided the answer. But fired by his failure – only just – to stop Earls crossing the line, Mike Phillips was determined to undo the damage.

The scrum half's try was the turning point of the game. Scooping the ball off the ground, Phillips escaped the grasp of Gordon D'Arcy and timed a blindside swallow dive as beautifully as Tom Daley to ground the ball before his ankles were yanked into touch.

Twelve thousand miles away, Phillips's defiant roar of celebration was echoed in living rooms and pub lounges across Wales. Our first semi-final for 24 years edged nearer but we weren't there yet. An increasingly rattled Ireland swapped their half backs but at just five points clear our anxiety levels hadn't dipped either as Priestland found the woodwork rather than the space between. However stronger Wales now seemed than Ireland's tiring stalwarts the scoreboard didn't reflect the gap. It took Jonathan Davies to widen it.

The ease with which he evaded five Emerald shirts, shrugging off Earls's tackle and palming off Cian Healy in the process, seemed to surprise even the Scarlets centre himself. As Priestland added the extras, breakfast bedlam erupted in The Conway.

Wales finished as they began, scintillating in attack, immense in defence and bubbling with a youthful brio that made them the best-loved team in the tournament.

Try scorer Jonathan Davies forces his way between Ireland's Sean O'Brien and Tommy Bowe

As England sloped out of the tournament facing a post-mortem on boorish behaviour and mediocre rugby, Wales's admirable team culture could not have been thrown into greater relief. We took as much pride in them as people as players, making their success even more satisfying.

Gatland's young braves were spreading their infectious brand of *hwyl* across the rugby world and beyond. From American rapper Snoop Dogg to *Gavin and Stacey*'s Essex boy Smithy, aka James Corden, everyone wanted to be Welsh that weekend.

I spoke to WRU president Dennis Gethin in what for him was the early hours of the morning and could hear the delight coming down the line from Wellington as he described how the players' ambassadorial conduct – as well as their play – has impressed everyone they have encountered.

'We're so proud of them. They were absolutely superb,' he said. 'And the most exciting thing about this team is they feel we haven't seen the best of them yet.'

With two matches between Wales and the Webb Ellis Trophy, what a wonderful thought that was.

October 10, 2011

. . . .

Journey's End as our Hearts break but swell with Pride

The day had come. Wales v France in the semi-final of the Rugby World Cup – the biggest opportunity in 130 years of Welsh rugby. The support was off the scale. Only a Welsh fan would carry his Dad's ashes around New Zealand so he 'could be there'. Only a Welsh fan would lie to his parents that his arm wasn't broken so he could still watch the semi-final, albeit in agony. And only 61,543 Welsh fans would turn up at the Millennium Stadium even though their heroes were 12,000 miles away.

October 15, 2011 **Wales 8 France 9**

When Sam Warburton upended Vincent Clerc, Alain Rolland turned our world upside down. A hemisphere away 61,543 fans had gathered in the Millennium Stadium determined to be Wales's 16th man. But their dreams of a world cup final were shattered when their team were cut to 14.

The most fervent supporters in world rugby bounced through the gates with 'Believe' written on their T-shirts. They left with disbelief etched on their faces.

Rolland's red card robbed Wales of their chance to achieve the greatest feat in the history of our game. The Irish ref with a French father also drained the colour from the tournament itself as a French side that lost to Tonga and weren't even rated by their own coach, progressed to the final.

A final that should have been ours, felt the men, women and children who turned the Millennium into match day minus grass and 30 players.

They streamed in at breakfast time fizzing with optimism. From toddlers wrapped in Welsh flags to pensioners in scarlet jerseys, thousands mingled, smiling at the novelty of it all. 'Eden Park is Millennium South,' one quipped, 'there's more of us here than there.'

Choosing their patch of concrete pitch, spreading into three tiers and taking their pick of the giant screens, they were delighted to embody the Max Boyce mantra of 'I Was There' – even thought their team weren't.

The media were out in force, chronicling an event that captured the imagination way beyond our borders. It seemed the ultimate feelgood story. If there's one nation on the planet that deserves the sporting success to match the passion of its people, it's surely Wales.

There were delightfully daft examples of that Cymric fanaticism dotted around the stadium. A trio of young women cross-dressed as the Welsh back row, complete with stubble and wigs, caught the lens of the cameras. 'Toby Faletau' – aka 24-year-old Natalie Guy from Cardiff – said the crowd were taking their cue from the attitude of Gatland's young side. 'As a team they're all so happy and united,' she said. 'They seem so at ease with one another. We love them.'

Stadium manager Gerry Toms – whose staff had sorted the logistics of the free screening with impressive speed – could barely believe the scale of the event he'd help create. Shaking his head incredulously at the scene unfolding before him, he said: 'We expected maybe 20,000 – and 20,000 tickets went in 25 minutes.' The final count revealed an astonishing total of 61,543 – 3,000 more than Eden Park.

Former Welsh international Emyr Lewis was similarly amazed by the biblical proportions of the crowd. 'Only in Wales,' he grinned, before admitting nervous anticipation was making his legs shake.

One supporter, however, was a picture of serenity. Postman Stephen Bennett – father of Welsh hooker Huw – had spent the week taking delivery of messages of support on every doorstep in Blaenau Gwent. And he was confident that a red letter day was on the cards for Wales. 'All the family are here,' he beamed. 'We're so proud of the boys – they've been ambassadors. I spoke to Huw last night. They're feeling good.'

And so were the fans. Led by Only Men Aloud and Tonypandy's West End starlet Sophie Evans, they sang the anthem as if willing their voices to travel 12,000 miles into the New Zealand night.

Even the early departure of Adam Jones couldn't puncture their bubble of belief. The first quarter confirmed what we'd all hoped – that in-form Wales were superior to flaky France. Which Les Blues had turned up? Not a side that matched our attacking intent by the looks of it.

But in the 18th minute Sam Warburton tip tackled Vincent Clerc and – although we didn't realise at that precise moment – our hopes of world cup glory crashed to the ground with the French winger.

Most of the Millennium masses assumed it was simply a sin-binning – and that felt bad enough. A buzz of analysis broke out. 'Not malicious was it? No intent there?' It took the heartbreaking sight of the red-eyed and red-carded captain filling the stadium's three huge screens to confirm the nation's worst nightmare. With more than 60 minutes of a world cup semi-final to go, Wales were without their most influential player.

There were tears and angry protestations before the decibel level dipped to a disgruntled murmur. I left my seat and took a shell-shocked walk into the corridor. Sam Our Captain, of all people. It felt like a sporting tragedy that could only befall Wales.

Finally, we had broken the cycle of heroic failure and were good enough to contend for the biggest prize only for the fates to intervene. With the cruellest of ironies, the young man who embodied everything that was good about this Welsh team – as a player and a person – had effectively ended Wales's chance of reaching the World Cup Final.

Letter of the law: Alain Rolland shows Warburton (obscured by Alun Wyn Jones, No 5) the red card

One rash decision from Rolland killed the dream. Why didn't he at least confer with his touchline assistant referees rather than reaching for red before the tackle was barely completed. Letter of the law maybe – what about the spirit of the game?

Our spirits, meanwhile, were on the floor. Only Men Aloud filled the half-time break with the cheery cheese of Journey's 'Don't Stop Believing' but many already had. How could Wales possibly survive with 14 men?

Yet as Gatland's young braves responded with the strength of character that has defined their world cup campaign, hope began to spread through the stands. They may have been 12,000 miles from Auckland but the fans roared every Welsh attack as if their heroes were within touching distance. When Mike Phillips burst around a scrum amd escaped the clutches of Pascal Pape to cross the line, utter delirium erupted.

Unconverted, the try wasn't enough to take the lead. The crowd ached for a drop goal as Stephen Jones came within range only for Wales to opt for more phases. With five minutes remaining, it was Leigh Halfpenny's turn to work a miracle from the halfway line. Some couldn't even bear to watch the young fullback take the kick. Those who did, thought he'd made it only for the replay to prompt a wail of disappointment.

And still Wales fought to the death, every player relentlessly pushing their bodies to the limit to compensate for their absent talisman. Dan Lydiate, Mike Phillips and Halfpenny in particular were outstanding while Jamie Roberts became a scrummaging forward as well as a maurading back.

Short of numbers on the field, Wales ran out of time on the clock with a phenomenal final flourish. Their home fans screamed their appreciation of every last one of those 27 phases. But it was not to be.

There were chances to be taken. Missed kicks cost Wales dearly. With 14 men, the game plan is distorted and the set-piece becomes an uneven contest. But to lose by a single point and prevent France from barely troubling Wales in their own 22 tells the story of the fightback that followed the ultimate setback.

The way Wales refused to unravel in the face of such misfortune will ensure their world cup semi-final goes down as one of the great acts of rugby courage. For the thousands spilling on to the streets of the Welsh capital, devastation was mixed with fierce pride.

As Julian Blamey, a supermarket worker from Porth, shepherded his young family down Westgate Street he paid tribute to Wales's performance: 'We were the better team even though we had 14 men. The red card was a very controversial decision – a yellow card would have been enough.

'But the event was brilliant, I brought my two children and my niece down and they've thoroughly enjoyed it. From the build-up, getting up early and getting excited, they really looked forward to it. And I can't fault the Millennium Stadium and the WRU for putting

· ·

the event on because the children have had such a great time. The result's so disappointing though. The expectation after the quarter finals was that we could have gone further.'

Paul Jones from Cardiff sympathised with the players: 'It's so gutting for the team. They've come so far to lose to a very average French team because of one decision on the day,' he said. 'Everyone was so buoyant on the way in and it looked as if it was going to be a comfortable win. To think we only lost by one point playing with 14 men for three quarters of the game. France didn't break our line. But let's concentrate on our lads. They're young and in four years time they'll be back.'

Diane Richards from Bassaleg praised Wales's resilience: '14 men played their hearts out. A lot of teams would have crumbled in that position but we didn't. I'm proud to be Welsh. They've had a brilliant world cup campaign. They've done amazingly to get to the semi-finals. We would have loved to get to the final but I am still really pleased for the boys.'

And while Alain Rolland may have judged Sam Warburton the villain of the piece, Diane was in no doubt what the Welsh captain means to his people. 'Sam is still our hero.'

His teammates were heroes too on a day when 61,543 hearts were both broken and swelling with pride.

October 17, 2012

The reason this Welsh team captured the hearts of so many people throughout the rugby world – impressing even the usually impervious host nation – is because they embodied the values of rugby itself. Sam Warburton's dignified acceptance of that dream-shattering red card summed up their collective character. The players know a great performance should not be confined to the field of play and representing your country does not end with the whistle.

So while we might have wanted a different result at the end of Wales's world cup journey, we couldn't have wished for better ambassadors. They didn't come home with a trophy or medals but in the greater scheme of things they won something just as precious – respect.

The 2011 Rugby World Cup also propelled a new and exciting generation of Welsh players onto the global stage. And just as I've loved recording the deeds of those who've gone before them so I look forward to chronicling the adventures of those who play in red in the years to come.